SUSE Manager 3 - Refernce Manual

A catalogue record for this book is available from the Hong Kong Public Libraries.

Published in Hong Kong by Samurai Media Limited.

Email: info@samuraimedia.org

ISBN 978-988-8406-64-7

Contents

About This Guide

SUSE® Manager enables you to efficiently manage a set of Linux systems and keep them up-to-date. It provides automated and cost-effective software management, asset management, system provisioning, and monitoring capabilities. SUSE Manager is compatible with Red Hat Satellite Server and offers seamless management of both SUSE® Linux Enterprise and Red Hat Enterprise Linux client systems.

This manual explains the features of the Web interface and is intended for SUSE Manager administrators and administrators with restricted roles for specific tasks. On certain topics we also provide background information, while some chapters contain links to additional documentation resources. The latter include additional documentation available on the installed system as well as documentation on the Internet.

For an overview of the documentation available for your product and the latest documentation updates, refer to http://www.suse.com/documentation/suse_manager/ or to the following section.

HTML versions of the manuals are also available from the *Help* tab of the SUSE Manager Web interface.

 Note: Obtaining the Release Notes

Although this manual reflects the most current information possible, read the *SUSE Manager Release Notes* for information that may not have been available prior to the finalization of the documentation. The notes can be found at http://www.suse.com/documentation/suse_manager/.

1 Available Documentation

The following manuals are available on this product:

SUSE Manager Quickstart

Lists installation scenarios and example topologies for different SUSE Manager setups. Guides you step by step through the installation, setup and basic configuration of SUSE Manager. Also contains detailed information about SUSE Manager maintenance and troubleshooting.

SUSE Manager Reference Manual

Reference documentation that covers the Web interface to SUSE Manager.

HTML versions of the product manuals can be found in the installed system under `/usr/share/` `doc/manual`. Find the latest documentation updates at http://www.suse.com/documentation where you can download PDF or HTML versions of the manuals for your product.

2 Feedback

Several feedback channels are available:

Bugs and Enhancement Requests

For services and support options available for your product, refer to http://www.suse.com/support/.

To report bugs for a product component, go to https://scc.suse.com/support/requests, log in, and click *Create New*.

User Comments

We want to hear your comments about and suggestions for this manual and the other documentation included with this product. Use the User Comments feature at the bottom of each page in the online documentation or go to http://www.suse.com/doc/feedback.html and enter your comments there.

Mail

For feedback on the documentation of this product, you can also send a mail to `doc-team@suse.de`. Make sure to include the document title, the product version and the publication date of the documentation. To report errors or suggest enhancements, provide a concise description of the problem and refer to the respective section number and page (or URL).

3 Documentation Conventions

The following typographical conventions are used in this manual:

- `/etc/passwd`: directory names and filenames.

- *placeholder*: replace *placeholder* with the actual value.

- `PATH`: the environment variable PATH.

- `ls`, `--help`: commands, options, and parameters.

- `user`: users or groups.

- `Alt`, `Alt`–`F1`: a key to press or a key combination; keys are displayed with uppercase letters as on a keyboard.

- *File*, *File* › *Save As*: menu items, buttons.

- `System z, ipseries` ❯ This paragraph is only relevant for the specified architectures. The arrows mark the beginning and the end of the text block. ◁

- *Dancing Penguins* (Chapter *Penguins*, ↑Another Manual): This is a reference to a chapter in another manual.

I Web Interface

1 Web Interface — Navigation and Overview

This is a chapter about the layout of the Web Interface to SUSE Manager and basic usage information.

1.1 Navigation

The top navigation bar is divided in a left and right part. The left part contains a row of tabs. SUSE Manager Administrators see *Figure 1.1, "Top Navigation Bar—SUSE Manager"* as the top navigation bar. Only SUSE Manager Administrators see the *Admin* tab.

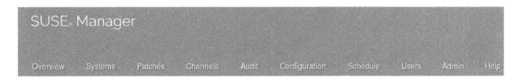

FIGURE 1.1: TOP NAVIGATION BAR—SUSE MANAGER

The left navigation bar is divided into pages. The links are context-sensitive. The *Figure 1.2, "Left Navigation Bar—Users"* is an example of the left navigation bar for the *Users* tab.

FIGURE 1.2: LEFT NAVIGATION BAR—USERS

Some pages have subtabs. These tabs offer an additional layer of granularity in performing tasks for systems or users. *Figure 1.3, "Subtabs—System Details"* is a menu bar for all *System Details* subtabs. This system has Management and Provisioning entitlements.

FIGURE 1.3: SUBTABS—SYSTEM DETAILS

The right part of the top navigation contains various functionality such a quick search, links to background information, user preferences, or sign off.

FIGURE 1.4: RIGHT PART OF THE TOP NAVIGATION BAR

1.1.1 Views Depending on User Roles

Keep in mind, since this guide covers the administrator user role level, some tabs, pages, and even whole categories described here may not be visible to you. Text markers are not used to identify, which functions are available to each user role level.

1.1.2 Categories and Pages

This section summarizes all of the categories and primary pages (those linked from the top and left navigation bars) within the SUSE Manager Web interface. It does not list the many subpages, tabs and subtabs accessible from the left navigation bar and individual pages. Each area of the Web interface is explained in detail later in this part.

- *Overview* — View and manage your primary account information and get help.

  - *Overview* — Obtain a quick overview of your account. This page notifies you if your systems need attention, provides a quick link directly to these systems, displays the most recent patch alerts for your account, and recently registered systems.

  - *Your Account* — Update your personal profile, addresses, email, and credentials. Deactivate your account.

  - *Your Preferences* — Indicate if you wish to receive email notifications about available patches for your systems. Set how many items are displayed in system and group lists. Set contents of the overview start page. Select your preferred CSV separator.

  - *Locale Preferences* — Configure timezone.

  - *Your Organization* — Update organization configuration and display organization trusts.

- *Systems* — Manage all your systems (including virtual guests) here.

- *Overview* — View a summary of your systems or system groups showing how many available patches each system has and which systems are entitled.

- *Systems* — Select and view subsets of your systems by specific criteria, such as Virtual Systems, Unentitled, Recently Registered, Proxy, and Inactive.

- *System Groups* — List your system groups. Create additional groups.

- *System Set Manager* — Perform various actions on sets of systems, including scheduling patch updates, package management, listing and creating new groups, managing channel entitlements, deploying configuration files, schedule audits, and check status.

- *Advanced Search* — Quickly search all your systems by specific criteria, such as name, hardware, devices, system info, networking, packages, and location.

- *Activation Keys* — Generate an activation key for a SUSE Manager-entitled system. This activation key can be used to grant a specific level of entitlement or group membership to a newly registered system using the `rhnreg_ks` command.

- *Stored Profiles* — View system profiles used to provision systems.

- *Custom System Info* — Create and edit system information keys with completely customizable values assigned while provisioning systems.

- *Autoinstallation* — Display and modify various aspects of autoinstallation profiles (Kickstart and AutoYaST) used in provisioning systems.

- *Software Crashes* — List software crashes grouped by UUID.

- *Virtual Host Managers* — Display and modify virtual host managers, file-based or VMware-based.

- *Salt* — View all minions. Manage onboarding, remote commands, and states catalogs.

  - *Onboarding* —

  - *Remote Commands* —

  - *States Catalog* —

- *Patches* — View and manage patch (errata) alerts here.

- *Patches* — Lists patch alerts and downloads associated RPMs relevant to your systems.

- *Advanced Search* — Search patch alerts based on specific criteria, such as synopsis, advisory type, and package name.

- *Manage Patches* — Manage the patches for an organization's channels.

- *Clone Patches* — Clone patches for an organization for ease of replication and distribution across an organization.

- *Channels* — View and manage the available SUSE Manager channels and the files they contain.

  - *Software Channels* — View a list of all software channels and those applicable to your systems.

  - *Package Search* — Search packages using all or some portion of the package name, description, or summary, with support for limiting searches to supported platforms.

  - *Manage Software Channels* — Create and edit channels used to deploy configuration files.

  - *Distribution Channel Mapping* — Define default base channels for servers according to their operating system or architecture when registering.

- *Audit* — View and search CVE audits and OpenSCAP scans.

  - *CVE Audit* — View a list of systems with their patch status regarding a given CVE (Common Vulnerabilities and Exposures) number.

  - *OpenSCAP* — View and search OpenSCAP scans.

- *Configuration* — Keep track of and manage configuration channels, actions, individual configuration files, and systems with SUSE Manager-managed configuration files.

  - *Overview* — A general dashboard view that shows a configuration summary.

  - *Configuration Channels* — List and create configuration channels from which any subscribed system can receive configuration files.

  - *Configuration Files* — List and create files from which systems receive configuration input.

  - *Systems* — List the systems that have SUSE Manager-managed configuration files.

- *Schedule* — Keep track of your scheduled actions.

  - *Pending Actions* — List scheduled actions that have not been completed.

  - *Failed Actions* — List scheduled actions that have failed.

  - *Completed Actions* — List scheduled actions that have been completed. Completed actions can be archived at any time.

  - *Archived Actions* — List completed actions that have been selected to archive.

  - *Action Chains* — View and edit defined action chains.

- *Users* — View and manage users in your organization.

  - *User List* — List users in your organization.

  - *System Group Configuration* — Configure user group creation.

- *Admin* (visible only to SUSE Manager administrators) — Use the Setup Wizard to configure SUSE Manager. List, create, and manage one or more SUSE Manager organizations. The SUSE Manager administrator can assign channel entitlements, create and assign administrators for each organization, and other tasks.

  - *Setup Wizard* — Streamlined configuration of basic tasks.

  - *Organizations* — List and create new organizations.

  - *Users* — List all users known by SUSE Manager, across all organizations. Click individual user names to change administrative privileges of the user.

     Note

    Users created for organization administration can only be configured by the organization administrator, *not* the SUSE Manager administrator.

  - *SUSE Manager Configuration* — Make General configuration changes to the SUSE Manager server, including Proxy settings, Certificate configuration, Bootstrap Script configuration, Organization changes, and Restart the SUSE Manager server.

  - *ISS Configuration* — Configure master and slave servers for inter-server synchronization.

- *Task Schedules* — View and create schedules.
- *Task Engine Status* — View the status of the various tasks of the SUSE Manager task engine.
  - *Show Tomcat Logs* — Display the log entries of the Tomcat server, on which the SUSE Manager server is running.
- *Help* — List references to available help resources.

1.1.3 Patch Alert Icons

Throughout SUSE Manager you will see three patch (errata) alert icons.

- 🛡 — represents a security alert.
- 🐞 — represents a bug fix alert.
- ➕ — represents an enhancement alert.

In the *Overview* page, click on the patch advisory to view details about the patch or click on the number of affected systems to see which are affected by the patch alert. Both links take you to tabs of the *Patch Details* page. Refer to *Section 4.2.2, "Patch Details"* for more information.

1.1.4 Quick Search

In addition to the Advanced Search functionality for Packages, Patches (Errata), Documentation, and Systems offered within some categories, SUSE Manager also offers a Quick Search tool near the top of each page. To use it, select the search item (choose from *Systems, Packages, Documentation,* and *Patches*) and type a keyword to look for a name match. Click the *Search* button. Your results appear at the bottom of the page.

FIGURE 1.5: QUICK SEARCH IN THE TOP NAVIGATION BAR

If you misspell a word during your search query, the SUSE Manager search engine performs approximate string (or fuzzy string) matching, returning results that may be similar in spelling to your misspelled queries.

For example, if you want to search for a certain development system called `test-1.example.com` that is registered with SUSE Manager, but you misspell your query `tset`, the `test-1.example.com` system still appears in the search results.

 Note

> If you add a distribution or register a system with a SUSE Manager server, it may take several minutes for it to be indexed and appear in search results.

- For advanced System searches, refer to *Section 2.6, "Advanced Search"*.

- For advanced Patch or Errata searches, refer to *Section 4.3, "Advanced Search"*.

- For advanced Package searches, refer to *Section 5.2, "Package Search"*.

- For advanced Documentation searches, refer to *Section 11.6, "Search"*.

1.1.5   Systems Selected

On the *System Overview* page, if you mark the check box next to a system, a tool for keeping track of the systems you have selected for use in the System Set Manager pops up on the top right corner. At any time, it identifies the number of selected systems and provides the means to work with them. Clicking the *Clear* button deselects all systems while clicking the *Manage* button launches the System Set Manager with your selected systems in place.

These systems can be selected in a number of ways. Only systems with at least a Management system role are eligible for selection. On all system and system group lists, a Select column exists for this purpose. Select the check boxes next to the systems or groups and click the *Update List* button below the column. Each time the Systems Selected tool at the top of the page changes to reflect the new number of systems ready for use in the System Set Manager. Refer to *Section 2.5, "System Set Manager"* for details.

1.1.6 Lists

The information within most categories is presented in the form of lists. These lists have some common features for navigation. For instance, you can navigate through virtually all lists by clicking the back and next arrows above and below the right side of the table. Some lists also offer the option to retrieve items alphabetically by clicking letters above the table.

 Note: Performing Large List Operations

Performing operations on large lists—such as removing RPM packages from the database with the SUSE Manager Web interface—may take some time and the system may become unresponsive or signal "Internal Server Error 500". Nevertheless, the command will succeed in the background if you wait long enough.

1.2 Overview

Entering the SUSE Manager URL in a browser takes you to the *Sign in* screen. If you click on the *About* tab before logging in, you will find documentation links, including a search function, and the option to request your login credentials if you forgot either password or login. Click on *Lookup Login/Password*.

 Note

If you forgot your password, enter your *SUSE Manager Login* and *Email Address* in the *Password Reset* section and click the *Send Password* button. Your password will be reset and sent to you. If you cannot remember your username, enter your *Email Address* in the *Login Information* section, then click on *Send Login*. Your username will be sent to you.

After logging into the Web interface of SUSE Manager, the first page to appear is *Overview*. This page contains important information about your systems, including summaries of system status, actions, and patch alerts.

 Note

If you are new to the SUSE Manager Web interface, read *Section 1.1, "Navigation"* to familiarize yourself with the layout and symbols used throughout the interface.

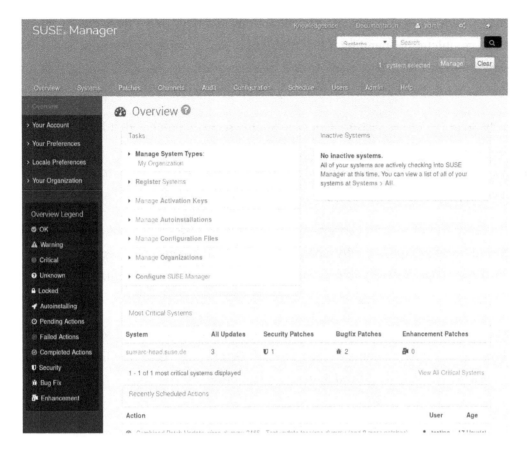

FIGURE 1.6: OVERVIEW

This page is split into functional areas, with the most critical areas displayed first. Users can control which of the following areas are displayed by making selections on the *Overview* › *Your Preferences* page. Refer to *Section 1.4, "Your Preferences"* for more information.

- The *Tasks* area lists the most common tasks an administrator performs via the web. Click any link to reach the page within SUSE Manager that allows you to accomplish that task.

- If any systems have not been checking in to SUSE Manager, they are listed under *Inactive System* to the right. Highlighting them in this way allows an administrator to quickly select those systems for troubleshooting.

- The *Most Critical Systems* section lists the most critical systems within your organization. It provides a link to quickly view those systems and displays a summary of the patch updates that have yet to be applied to those systems. Click the name of the system to see its *System Details* page and apply the patch updates. Below the list is a link to *View All Critical Systems* on one page.

- The *Recently Scheduled Actions* section lists all actions less than thirty days old and their status: failed, completed, or pending. Click the label of any given action to view its details page. Below the list is a link to *View All Scheduled Actions* on one page, which lists all actions that have not yet been carried out on your client systems.

- The *Relevant Security Patches* section lists all available security patches that have yet to be applied to some or all of your client systems. It is critical that you apply these security patches to keep your systems secure. Below this list find links to all patches (*View All Patches*) and to the patches that apply to your systems (*View All Relevant Patches*).

- The *System Group Names* section lists groups you may have created and indicates whether the systems in those groups are fully updated. Click the link below this section to get to the *System Groups* page, where you can choose *System Groups* to use with the System Set Manager.

- The *Recently Registered Systems* section lists the systems added to the SUSE Manager in the past 30 days. Click a system's name to see its *System Details* page. Click the link below this section to *View All Recently Registered Systems* on one page.

To return to this page, click *Overview* on the left navigation bar.

1.3 Your Account

On the *Your Account* page modify your personal information, such as name, password, and title. To modify any of this information, make the changes in the appropriate text fields and click the *Update* button at the bottom.

If you change your SUSE Manager password, for security reasons you will not see the new password while you enter it. Replace the asterisks in the *Password* and *Confirm Password* text fields with the new password.

 Note

> Should you forget your password or username, go to the login screen and click the *About* tab, then select the *Lookup Login/Password* page. Here you can either specify your login and email address or only your email address if you are not sure about the username. Then click on *Send Password* or *Send Login* respectively.

1.3.1 Addresses

On the *Addresses* page manage your mailing, billing and shipping addresses, and the associated phone numbers. Click *Edit this address* below the address to be modified, make the changes, and click *Update*.

1.3.2 Change Email

The email address listed in the *Your Account* page is the address to which SUSE Manager sends email notifications if you select to receive patch alerts or daily summaries for your systems on the *Your Preferences* page.

To change your preferred email address, click *Change Email* in the left navigation bar. Enter your new email address and click the *Update* button. A confirmation email is sent to the new email address; responding to the confirmation email validates the new email address. Invalid email addresses like those ending in `@localhost` are filtered and rejected.

1.3.3 Credentials

View or enter external system or API credentials associated with your SUSE Manager account, for example your SUSE Studio credentials.

1.3.4 Account Deactivation

The *Account Deactivation* page provides a means to cancel your SUSE Manager service. To do so, click the *Deactivate Account* button. The Web interface returns you to the login screen. If you attempt to log back in, an error message advises you to contact the SUSE Manager administrator for your organization. Note that if you are the only SUSE Manager Administrator for your organization, you are unable to deactivate your account.

1.4 Your Preferences

The *Your Preferences* page allows you to configure SUSE Manager options, including:

- *Email Notifications* — Determine whether you want to receive email every time a patch alert is applicable to one or more systems in your account.

   Important

  This setting also enables Management and Provisioning customers to receive a daily summary of system events. These include actions affecting packages, such as scheduled patches, system reboots, or failures to check in. In addition to selecting this check box, you must identify each system to be included in this summary email. By default, all Management and Provisioning systems are included in the summary. Add more systems either individually on the *System Details* page or for multiple systems at once in the *System Set Manager* interface. Note that SUSE Manager sends these summaries only to verified email addresses. To disable all messages, simply deselect this check box.

- *SUSE Manager List Page Size* — Maximum number of items that appear in a list on a single page. If more items are in the list, clicking the *Next* button displays the next group of items. This preference applies to system lists, patch lists, package lists, and so on.

- *"Overview" Start Page* — Select the information areas that are displayed on the *Overview* Start Page. Check the box to the left of the information area you would like to include.

- *CSV Files* — Select the separator character to be used in downloadable CSV files. *Comma* is the default; as an alternative use *Semicolon*, which is more compatible with Microsoft Excel.

After making changes to any of these options, click the *Save Preferences* button.

1.5 Locale Preferences

On the *Overview > Locale Preferences* page set your SUSE Manager interface to your local time by selecting the appropriate *Time Zone* from the drop-down box, then click the *Save Preferences* button to apply the selection.

1.6 Your Organization

On the *Your Organization* page modify your organization's *Configuration* and the *Organization Trusts*.

1.6.1 Configuration

On the *Configuration* page modify your personal information, such as name, password, and title. To modify any of this information, make the changes in the appropriate text fields and click the *Update* button at the bottom.

1.6.2 Organization Trusts

The *Organization Trusts* page displays the trusts established with your organization (that is, the organization with which you, the logged-in user, are associated). The page also lists *Channels Shared*, which refers to channels available to your organization via others in the established trusts.

You can filter the list of trusts by keyword using the *Filter by Organization* text box and clicking *Go*.

2 Systems

If you click the *Systems* tab on the top navigation bar, the *Systems* category and links appear. Here you can select systems to perform actions on them and create system profiles.

2.1 Overview

The *Overview* page provides a summary of your systems, including their status, number of associated patches (errata) and packages, and their so-called system type. Clicking on the name of a system takes you to its *System Details* page. Refer to *Section 2.3, "System Details"* for more information.

Clicking *View System Groups* at the top of the *Overview* page takes you to a similar summary of your system groups. It identifies group status and displays the number of systems contained. Clicking on the number of systems takes you to the *Systems* tab of the *System Group Details* page, while clicking on the system name takes you to the *Details* tab for that system. Refer to *Section 2.4.3, "System Group Details"* for more information.

You can also click on *Use in SSM* in the *System Groups* section to go directly to the *System Set Manager*. Refer to *Section 2.5, "System Set Manager"* for more information.

2.2 Systems

The *Systems* page displays a list of all your registered systems. Several columns provide information for each system:

- *Select*: Systems with a system tye cannot be selected. To select systems, mark the appropriate check boxes. Selected systems are added to the *System Set Manager*, where actions can be carried out simultaneously on all systems in the set. Refer to *Section 2.5, "System Set Manager"* for details.

- *System*: The name of the system specified during registration. The default name is the hostname of the system. Clicking on the name of a system displays its *System Details* page. Refer to *Section 2.3, "System Details"* for more information.

- *Updates*: Shows which type of update action is applicable to the system or confirms that the system is up-to-date. Some icons are linked to related tasks. For instance, the standard Updates icon is linked to the *Upgrade* subtab of the packages list, while the Critical Updates icon links directly to the *Software Patches* page where you can *Apply Patches*. The Not Checking In icon is linked to instructions for resolving the issue.

  - — System is up-to-date.

  - — Critical patch (errata) available, update *strongly* recommended.

  - — Updates available and recommended.

  - — System not checking in properly (for 24 hours or more).

  - — System is locked; actions prohibited.

  - — System is being deployed using AutoYaST or Kickstart.

  - — Updates have been scheduled.

  - — System not entitled to any update service.

- *Patches* — Total number of patch alerts applicable to the system.

- *Packages*: Total number of package updates for the system, including packages related to patch alerts as well as newer versions of packages not related to patch alerts. For example, if a client system that has an earlier version of a package installed gets subscribed to the appropriate base channel of SUSE Manager (such as SUSE Linux Enterprise 12 SP1), that channel may have an updated version of the package. If so, the package appears in the list of available package updates.

  Important

  If SUSE Manager identifies package updates for the system, but the package updater (such as Red Hat Update Agent or YaST) responds with a message like "Your system is fully updated", a conflict likely exists in the system's package profile or in the up2date configuration file. To resolve the conflict, either schedule a package list update or remove the packages from the package exceptions list. Refer to *Section 2.3, "System Details"* for instructions.

- *Configs*: Total number of configuration files applicable to the system.

- *Crashes*:

- *Base Channel*: The primary channel for the system based on its operating system. Refer to *Section 5.1, "Software Channels"* for more information.

- *System Type*: Shows whether or not the system is manageed and at what service level.

Links in the left navigation bar below *Systems* enable you to select and view predefined sets of your systems. All of the options described above can be applied within these pages.

2.2.1 All

The *All* page contains the default set of your systems. It displays every system you have permission to manage. You have permission if you are the only user in your organization, if you are a SUSE Manager Administrator, or if the system belongs to a group for which you have admin rights.

2.2.2 Physical Systems

To reach this page, select the *Systems* tab, followed by the *Systems* subtab from the left navigation bar, and finally select *Physical Systems* from the left navigation bar. This page lists each physical system of which SUSE Manager is aware.

2.2.3 Virtual Systems

To reach this page, select the *Systems* tab, followed by the *Systems* subtab from the left navigation bar, and finally select *Virtual Systems* from the left navigation bar. This page lists each virtual host of which SUSE Manager is aware and the guest systems on those hosts.

System

This column displays the name of each guest system.

Updates

This column shows whether there are patches (errata updates) available for the guest systems that have not yet been applied.

Status

This column indicates whether a guest is running, paused, or stopped.

Base Channel

This column displays the base channel to which the guest is currently subscribed.

Only guests registered with SUSE Manager are displayed with blue text. Clicking on the hostname of such a guest system displays its *System Details* page.

2.2.4   Bare Metal Systems

Here, all unprovisioned (bare-metal) systems with hardware details are listed. For more information on bare-metal systems, see *Section 10.4.6, "Admin > SUSE Manager Configuration > Bare-metal systems"*.

2.2.5   Out of Date

The *Out of Date* page displays all systems where applicable patch alerts have not been applied.

2.2.6   Requiring Reboot

Systems listed here need rebooting. Click on the name for details, where you can also schedule a reboot.

2.2.7   Non-compliant Systems

Non-compliant systems have packages installed which are not available from SUSE Manager. *Packages* shows how many installed packages are not available in the channels assigned to the system. A non-compliant system cannot be reinstalled.

2.2.8 Without System Type

The *Without System Type* page displays systems that have ...

2.2.9 Ungrouped

The *Ungrouped* page displays systems not yet assigned to a specific system group.

2.2.10 Inactive

The *Inactive* page displays systems that have not checked in with SUSE Manager for 24 hours or more. Checking in means that the Red Hat Update Agent on Red Hat Enterprise Linux or the YaST Online Update on SUSE Linux Enterprise client systems connects to SUSE Manager to see if there are any updates available or if any actions have been scheduled. If you see a message telling you that check-ins are not taking place, the client system is not successfully connecting to SUSE Manager. The reason may be one of the following:

- The system is not entitled to any SUSE Manager service. System profiles that remain unentitled for 180 days (6 months) are removed.

- The system is entitled, but the SUSE Manager daemon (`rhnsd`) has been disabled on the system.

- The system is behind a firewall that does not allow connections over `https` (port 443).

- The system is behind an HTTP proxy server that has not been properly configured.

- The system is connected to a SUSE Manager Proxy Server or SUSE Manager that has not been properly configured.

- The system itself has not been properly configured, perhaps pointing at the wrong SUSE Manager Server.

- The system is not in the network.

- Some other barrier exists between the system and the SUSE Manager Server.

2.2.11 Recently Registered

The *Recently Registered* page displays any systems that have been registered in a given period. Use the drop-down menu to specify the period in days, weeks, 30- and 180-day increments, and years.

2.2.12 Proxy

The *Proxy* page displays the SUSE Manager Proxy Server systems registered with your SUSE Manager server.

2.2.13 Duplicate Systems

The *Duplicate Systems* page lists current systems and any active and inactive entitlements associated with them. Active entitlements are in gray, while inactive entitlements are highlighted in yellow and their check boxes checked by default for you to delete them as needed by clicking the *Delete Selected* button. Entitlements are inactive if the system has not checked in with SUSE Manager in a time specified via the drop-down list *A system profile is inactive if its system has not checked in for:*.

You can filter duplicate entitlements by *IP Address, Hostname,* or *MAC address* by clicking on the respective subtab. You may filter further by inactive time or typing the system's hostname, IP address, or MAC address in the corresponding *Filter by:* text box.

To compare up to three duplicate entitlements at one time, click the *Compare Systems* link in the *Last Checked In* column. Inactive components of the systems are highlighted in yellow. You can then determine which systems are inactive or duplicate and delete them by clicking the *Delete System Profile* button. Click the *Confirm Deletion* button to confirm your choice.

2.2.14 System Currency

The System Currency Report displays an overview of severity scores of patches relevant to the system. The weighting is defined via the *System Details* page. The default weight awards critical security patches with the heaviest weight and enhancements with the lowest. The report can be used to prioritize maintenance actions on the systems registered to SUSE Manager.

2.2.15 System Types

System Types define the set of functionalities available for each system in SUSE Manager such as the ability of installing software or creating guest virtual machines.

A list of profiled systems follows, with their base and add-on system types shown in the appropriate columns. To change system types, select the systems you wish to modify, and choose either *Add System Type* or *Remove System Type*

2.3 System Details

Once systems are registered to SUSE Manager, they are displayed on the *Systems* › *Overview* page. Here and on any other page, clicking the name takes you to the *System Details* page of the client, where all kinds of administrative tasks can be performed, including the removal of a system.

 Note

> The *Delete System* link in the upper right of this screen refers to the system profile only. Deleting a host system profile will not destroy or remove the registration of guest systems. Deleting a guest system profile does not remove it from the list of guests for its host, nor does it stop or pause the guest. It does, however, remove your ability to manage it via SUSE Manager.
>
> If you mistakenly deleted a system profile from SUSE Manager, you may re-register the system using the bootstrap script or **rhnreg_ks** manually.

The Details page has numerous subtabs that provide specific system information as well as other identifiers unique to the system. The following sections discuss these tabs and their subtabs in detail.

2.3.1 System Details > Details

This page is not accessible from any of the standard navigation bars. However, clicking on the name of a system anywhere in the Web interface displays this page. By default the *Details* › *Overview* subtab is displayed. Other tabs are available, depending on the system type and add-on system type.

2.3.1.1   System Details > Details > Overview

This system summary page displays the system status message and the following key information about the system:

SYSTEM STATUS

This message indicates the current state of your system in relation to SUSE Manager.

 Note

If updates are available for any entitled system, the message *Software Updates Available* appears, displaying the number of critical and non-critical updates as well as the sum of affected packages. To apply these updates, click on *Packages* and select some or all packages to update, then click *Upgrade Packages*.

SYSTEM INFO

Hostname

The hostname as defined by the client system.

IP Address

The IP address of the client.

IPv6 Address

The IPv6 address of the client.

Virtualization

If the client is a virtual machine, the type of virtualization is listed.

UUID

Displays the universally unique identifier.

Kernel

The kernel installed and operating on the client system.

SUSE Manager System ID

A unique identifier generated each time a system registers with SUSE Manager.

Note

The system ID can be used to eliminate duplicate profiles from SUSE Manager. Compare the system ID listed on this page with the information stored on the client system in the `/etc/sysconfig/rhn/systemid` file. In that file, the system's current ID is listed under `system_id`. The value starts after the characters `ID-`. If the value stored in the file does not match the value listed in the profile, the profile is not the most recent one and may be removed.

Activation Key

Displays the activation key used to register the system.

Installed Products

Lists the products installed on the system.

Lock Status

Indicates whether a system has been locked.

Actions cannot be scheduled for locked systems on the Web interface until the lock is removed manually. This does not include preventing automated patch updates scheduled via the Web interface. To prevent the application of automated patch updates, deselect *Auto Patch Update* from the *System Details* › *Details* › *Properties* subtab. For more information, refer to *Section 2.3.1.2, " System Details > Details > Properties "*.

Locking a system can prevent you from accidentally changing a system. For example, the system may be a production system that should not receive updates or new packages until you decide to unlock it.

 Important

Locking a system in the Web interface *will not* prevent any actions that originate from the client system. For example, if a user logs into the client directly and runs YaST Online Update (on SLE) or **pup** (on RHEL), the update tool will install available patches whether or not the system is locked in the Web interface.

Locking a system *does not* restrict the number of users who can access the system via the Web interface. If you wish to restrict access to the system, associate that system with a System Group and assign a System Group Administrator to it. Refer to *Section 2.4, "System Groups"* for more information about System Groups.

It is also possible to lock multiple systems via the System Set Manager. Refer to *Section 2.5.10.4, " System Set Manager > Misc > Lock/Unlock "* for instructions.

SUBSCRIBED CHANNELS

List of subscribed channels. Clicking on a channel name takes you to the *Basic Channel Details* page. To change subscriptions, click the *(Alter Channel Subscriptions)* link right beside the title to assign available base and child channels to this system. When finished making selections, click the *Change Subscriptions* button to change subscriptions and the base software channel. For more information, refer to *Section 2.3.2.3, " System Details > Software > Software Channels "*.

Base Channel

The first line indicates the base channel to which this system is subscribed. The base channel should match the operating system of the client.

Child Channels

The subsequent lines of text, which depend on the base channel, list child channels. An example is the *SUSE Manager Tools* channel.

SYSTEM EVENTS

Checked In

The date and time at which the system last checked in with SUSE Manager.

Registered

The date and time at which the system registered with SUSE Manager and created this profile.

Last Booted

The date and time at which the system was last started or restarted.

 Note

Systems with a Management entitlement can be rebooted from this screen.

1. Select *Schedule system reboot.*

2. Provide the earliest date and time at which the reboot may take place.

3. Click the *Schedule Reboot* button in the lower right.

When the client checks in after the scheduled start time, SUSE Manager will instruct the system to restart itself.

OSA status is also displayed for client systems registered with SUSE Manager that have the OSA dispatcher (osad) configured.

Push enables SUSE Manager customers to immediately initiate tasks rather than wait for those systems to check in with SUSE Manager. Scheduling actions through push is identical to the process of scheduling any other action, except that the task can immediately be carried out instead of waiting the set interval for the system to check in.

In addition to the configuration of SUSE Manager, each client system to receive pushed actions must have the osad package installed and its service started.

SYSTEM PROPERTIES

System Types

Lists system types and add-on types currently applied to the system.

Notifications

Indicates the notification options for this system. You can choose whether you wish to receive email notifying you of available updates for this system. In addition, you may choose to include systems in the daily summary email.

Contact Method

Available methods: Pull, Push via SSH, and Push via SSH tunnel.

Auto Patch Update

Indicates whether this system is configured to accept updates automatically.

System Name

By default, the hostname of the client is displayed, but a different system name can be assigned.

Description

This information is automatically generated at registration. You can edit the description to include any information you wish.

Location

This field displays the physical address of the system if specified.

Clicking the *Edit These Properties* link right beside the *System Properties* title opens the *System Details › Properties* subtab. On this page, edit any text you choose, then click the *Update Properties* button to confirm.

2.3.1.2   System Details > Details > Properties

This subtab allows you to alter the following basic properties of your system:

SYSTEM DETAILS

System Name

By default, this is the hostname of the system. You can however alter the profile name to anything that allows you to distinguish this system from others.

Base System Type

Select one of the available base system types.

Add-on System Types

Notifications

Select whether notifications about this system should be sent and whether to include this system in the daily summary. This setting keeps you aware of all advisories pertaining to the system. Anytime an update is released for the system, you receive an email notification. The daily summary reports system events that affect packages, such as scheduled patch updates, system reboots, or failures to check in. In addition to including the system here, you must choose to receive email notification in the *Your Preferences* page of the *Overview* category.

Contact Method

Select between *Pull, Push via SSH*, and *Push via SSH tunnel*.

Auto Patch Update

If this box is checked, available patches are automatically applied to the system when it checks in (Pull) or immediately if you select either Push option. This action takes place without user intervention. The SUSE Manager Daemon (`rhnsd`) must be enabled on the system for this feature to work.

Note: Conflicts With Third Party Packages

Enabling auto-update might lead to failures because of conflicts between system updates and third party packages. To avoid failures caused by those issues, it is better to leave this box unchecked.

Description

By default, this text box records the operating system, release, and architecture of the system when it first registers. Edit this information to include anything you like.

The remaining fields record the physical address at which the system is stored. To confirm any changes to these fields, click the *Update Properties* button.

 Note: Setting Properties for Multiple Systems

Many of these properties can be set for multiple systems in one go via the System Set Manager interface. For details, see *Section 2.5, "System Set Manager"*.

2.3.1.3 System Details > Details > Remote Command

This subtab allows you to run a remote command on the system. Before doing so, you must first configure the system to accept such commands.

1. On SLE clients, subscribe the system to the SUSE Manager Tools child channel and use **zypper** to install the **rhncfg**, **rhncfg-client**, and **rhncfg-actions** packages, if not already installed:

   ```
   zypper in rhncfg rhncfg-client rhncfg-actions
   ```

   On RHEL clients, subscribe the system to the Tools child channel and use **up2date** or **yum** to install the **rhncfg**, **rhncfg-client**, and **rhncfg-actions** packages, if not already installed:

   ```
   yum install rhncfg rhncfg-client rhncfg-actions
   ```

2. Log into the system as root and add the following file to the local SUSE Manager configuration directory: `allowed-actions/scripts/run`.

a. Create the necessary directory on the target system:

```
mkdir -p /etc/sysconfig/rhn/allowed-actions/script
```

b. Create an empty run file in that directory to act as a flag to SUSE Manager, signaling permission to allow remote commands:

```
touch /etc/sysconfig/rhn/allowed-actions/script/run
```

Once the setup is complete, refresh the page in order to view the text fields for remote commands. Identify a specific user, group, and timeout period, as well as the script to run. Select a date and time to execute the command, then click *Schedule* or add the remote command to an action chain. For further information on action chains, refer to *Section 8.5, "Action Chains"*.

2.3.1.4 System Details > Details > Reactivation

Reactivation keys include this system's ID, history, groups, and channels. This key can then be used only once with the **rhnreg_ks** command line utility to re-register this system and regain all SUSE Manager settings. Unlike typical activation keys, which are not associated with a specific system ID, keys created here do not show up within the *Activation Keys* page.

Reactivation keys can be combined with activation keys to aggregate the settings of multiple keys for a single system profile. For example:

```
rhnreg_ks --server=server-url \
  --activationkey=reactivation-key,activationkey --force
```

 Warning

When autoinstalling a system with its existing SUSE Manager profile, the profile uses the system-specific activation key created here to re-register the system and return its other SUSE Manager settings. For this reason, you should not regenerate, delete, or use this key (with **rhnreg_ks**) while a profile-based autoinstallation is in progress. If you do, the autoinstallation will fail.

2.3.1.5   System Details > Details > Hardware

This subtab provides detailed information about the system, including networking, BIOS, memory, and other devices but only if you included the hardware profile for this machine during registration. If the hardware profile looks incomplete or outdated, click the *Schedule Hardware Refresh* button. The next time the SUSE Manager Daemon (`rhnsd`) connects to SUSE Manager, it will update your system profile with the latest hardware information.

2.3.1.6   System Details > Details > Migrate

This subtab provides the option to migrate systems between organizations. Select an *Organization Name* and click *Migrate System* to initiate the migration.

 Note

> Defined system details such as channel assignments, system group membership, custom data value, configuration channels, reactivation keys, and snapshots will be dropped from the system configuration after the migration.

2.3.1.7   System Details > Details > Notes

This subtab provides a place to create notes about the system. To add a new note, click the *Create Note* link, type a subject and write your note, then click the *Create* button. To modify a note, click on its subject in the list of notes, make your changes, and click the *Update* button. To remove a note, click on its subject in the list of notes then click the *delete note* link.

2.3.1.8   System Details > Details > Custom Info

This subtab provides completely customizable information about the system. Unlike *Notes*, *Custom Info* is structured, formalized, and can be searched. Before you can provide custom information about a system, you must have *Custom Information Keys*. Click on *Custom System Info* in the left navigation bar. Refer to *Section 2.9, "Custom System Info"* for instructions.

Once you have created one or more keys, you may assign values for this system by selecting the *Create Value* link. Click the name of the key in the resulting list and enter a value for it in the *Description* field, then click the *Update Key* button.

2.3.1.9   System Details > Details > Proxy

This tab is only available for SUSE Manager Proxy systems and lists all clients registered with the selected SUSE Manager Proxy server.

2.3.2   System Details > Software

This tab and its subtabs allow you to manage the software on the system: patches (errata), packages and package profiles, software channel memberships, and service pack (SP) migrations.

2.3.2.1   System Details > Software > Patches

This subtab contains a list of patch (errata) alerts applicable to the system. Refer to *Section 1.1.3, "Patch Alert Icons"* for meanings of the icons on this tab. To apply updates, select them and click the *Apply Patches* button. Double-check the updates to be applied on the confirmation page, then click the *Confirm* button. The action is added to the *Pending Actions* list under *Schedule*. Patches that have been scheduled cannot be selected for update. Instead of a check box there is a clock icon. Click on the clock to see the *Action Details* page.

A *Status* column in the patches table shows whether an update has been scheduled. Possible values are: None, Pending, Picked Up, Completed, and Failed. This column displays only the latest action related to a patch. For instance, if an action fails and you reschedule it, this column shows the status of the patch as `Pending` with no mention of the previous failure. Clicking a status other than `None` takes you to the *Action Details* page. This column corresponds to the one on the *Affected Systems* tab of the *Patch Details* page.

2.3.2.2   System Details > Software > Packages

Manage the software packages on the system. Most of the following actions can also be performed via action chains. For further information on action chains, refer to *Section 8.5, "Action Chains"*.

 Warning

When new packages or updates are installed on the client via SUSE Manager, any licenses (EULAs) requiring agreement before installation are automatically accepted.

Packages

The default display of the *Packages* tab describes the options available and provides the means to update your package list. To update or complete a potentially outdated list, possibly due to the manual installation of packages, click the *Update Package List* button in the bottom right-hand corner of this page. The next time the SUSE Manager daemon (`rhnsd`) connects to SUSE Manager, it updates your system profile with the latest list of installed packages.

List/Remove

Lists installed packages and enables you to remove them. View and sort packages by name, architecture, and the date they were installed on the system. Search for the desired packages by typing its name in the *Filter by Package Name* text box, or by clicking the letter or number corresponding to the first character of the package name. Click on a package name to view its *Package Details* page. To delete packages from the system, select their check boxes and click the *Remove Packages* button on the bottom right-hand corner of the page. A confirmation page appears with the packages listed. Click the *Confirm* button to remove the packages.

Upgrade

Displays a list of packages with newer versions available in the subscribed channels. Click on the latest package name to view its *Package Details* page. To upgrade packages immediately, select them and click the *Upgrade Packages* button. Any EULAs will be accepted automatically.

Install

Install new packages on the system from the available channels. Click on the package name to view its *Package Details* page. To install packages, select them and click the *Install Selected Packages* button. EULAs are automatically accepted.

Verify

Validates the packages installed on the system against its RPM database. This is the equivalent of running `rpm -V`. The metadata of the system's packages are compared with information from the database, such as file checksum, file size, permissions, owner, group and type. To verify a package or packages, select them, click the *Verify Selected Packages* button, and confirm. When the check is finished, select this action in the *History* subtab under *Events* to see the results.

Lock

Locking a package prevents modifications like removal or update of the package. Since locking and unlocking happens via scheduling requests, locking might take effect with some delay. If an update happens before then, the lock will have no effect. Select the packages you want to lock. If locking should happen later, select the date and time above the *Request Lock* button, then click on it. A small lock icon marks locked packages. To unlock, select the package and click *Request Unlock*, optionally specifying the date and time for unlocking to take effect.

 Note

This feature only works if Zypper is used as package manager. On the target machine the `zypp-plugin-spacewalk` package, version 0.96 or higher, must be installed.

Profiles

Compare installed packages with the package lists in stored profiles and other systems. Select a stored profile from the drop-down menu and click the *Compare* button. To compare with packages installed on a different system, select the system from the associated drop-down menu and click the *Compare* button. To create a stored profile based on the existing system, click the *Create System Profile* button, enter any additional information you desire, and click the *Create Profile* button. These profiles are kept within the *Stored Profiles* page linked from the left navigation bar.

Once installed packages have been compared with a profile, customers have the option to synchronize the selected system with the profile. All changes apply to the system not the profile. Packages might get deleted and additional packages installed on the system. To install only specific packages, click the respective check boxes in the profile. To remove specific packages installed on the system, select the check boxes of these packages showing a difference of *This System Only*. To completely synchronize the system's packages with the compared profile, select the master check box at the top of the column. Then click the *Sync Packages to* button. On the confirmation screen, review the changes, select a time frame for the action, and click the *Schedule Sync* button.

Non Compliant

    Lists packages that are installed on this system and are not present in any of its channels.

2.3.2.3   System Details > Software > Software Channels

Software channels provide a well-defined method to determine which packages should be available to a system for installation or upgrade based on its operating systems, installed packages, and functionality. Click a channel name to view its *Channel Details* page. To modify the child channels associated with this system, use the check boxes next to the channels and click the *Change Subscriptions* button. You will receive a success message or be notified of any errors. To change the system's base channel, select the new one from the drop-down menu and confirm. Refer to *Section 5.1, "Software Channels"* for more information.

2.3.2.4   System Details > Software > SP Migration

Service Pack Migration (SP Migration) means upgrading a system from one service pack level to next level.

 Warning

    During migration SUSE Manager automatically accepts any required licenses (EULAs) before installation.

SUSE only supports one step at a time, this means it is not be possible to migrate from e.g., SP1 to SP3. Supported migration paths include:

- SLES 11 SP1 → SLES 11 SP2 → SLES 11 SP3 → SLES 11 SP4

- SLES 12 → SLES 12 SP1

- SUSE Manager Proxy 1.2 → SUSE Manager Proxy 1.7

 Warning: Rollback Not Possible

    The migration feature does not cover any rollback functionality. Once the migration procedure is started, rolling back is not possible. Therefore it is recommended to have a working system backup available for an emergency.

2.3.2.5 System Details > Software > Software Crashes

Red Hat clients can be configured to report software failures to SUSE Manager via the Automatic Bug Reporting Tool (ABRT) to extend the overall reporting functionality of your systems. This functionality is not supported on SUSE Linux Enterprise systems. If configured appropriately, Red Hat clients automatically report software failures captured by ABRT and process the captured failures in a centralized fashion on SUSE Manager. You can use either the Web interface or the API to process these failure reports.

2.3.3 System Details > Configuration

This tab and its subtabs assist in managing the configuration files associated with the system. These configuration files may be managed solely for the current system or distributed widely via a Configuration Channel. The following sections describe these and other available options on the *System Details › Configuration* subtabs.

 Note

> To manage the configuration of a system, it must have the latest `rhncfg*` packages installed. Refer to *Section 7.1, "Preparing Systems for Config Management"* for instructions on enabling and disabling scheduled actions for a system.

This section is available to normal users with access to systems that have configuration management enabled. Like software channels, configuration channels store files to be installed on systems. While software updates are provided by SCC, configuration files are managed solely by you. Also unlike with software packages, various versions of configuration files may prove useful to a system at any given time. Only the latest version can be deployed.

2.3.3.1 System Details > Configuration > Overview

This subtab provides access to the configuration files of your system and to the most common tasks used to manage configuration files. In the *Configuration Overview*, click on the blue links to add files, directories, or symlinks. Here you also find shortcuts to perform any of the common configuration management tasks listed on the right of the screen by clicking one of the links under *Configuration Actions*.

2.3.3.2 System Details > Configuration > View/Modify Files

This subtab lists all configuration files currently associated with the system. These are sorted via subtabs in centrally and locally managed files and a local sandbox for files under development.

Centrally-Managed Files

> Centrally-managed configuration files are provided by global configuration channels. Determine which channel provides which file by examining the *Provided By* column below. Some of these centrally-managed files may be overridden by locally-managed files. Check the *Overridden By* column to find out if any files are overridden.

Locally-Managed Files

> Locally-managed configuration files are useful for overriding centrally-managed configuration profiles that cause problems on particular systems. Also, locally-managed configuration files are a method by which system group administrators who do not have configuration administration privileges can manage configuration files on the machines they are able to manage.

Local Sandbox

> In the sandbox you can store configuration files under development. You can promote files from the sandbox to a centrally-managed configuration channel using *Copy Latest to Central Channel*. After files in this sandbox have been promoted to a centrally-managed configuration channel, you will be able to deploy them to other systems.

2.3.3.3 System Details > Configuration > Add Files

To upload, import or create new configuration files, click on *Add Files*.

Upload File

> To upload a configuration file from your local machine, browse for the upload file, specify whether it is a text or binary file, enter *Filename/Path* as well as user and group ownership. Specific file permissions can be set. When done, click *Upload Configuration File*.

Import Files

> Via the *Import Files* tab, you can add files from the system you have selected before and add it to the sandbox of this system. Files will be imported the next time `rhn_check` runs on the system. To deploy these files or override configuration files in global channels, copy this file into your local override channel after the import has occurred.

In the text field under *Import New Files* enter the full path of any files you want import into SUSE Manager or select deployable configuration files from the *Import Existing Files* list. When done, click *Import Configuration Files*.

Create File

Under *Create File*, you can directly create the configuration file from scratch. Select the file type, specify the path and filename, where to store the file, plus the symbolic link target filename and path. Ownership and permissions as well as macro delimiters need to be set. For more information on using macros, see *Section 7.4.3, "Including Macros in your Configuration Files"*. In the *File Contents* text field, type the configuration file. Select the type of file you are creating from the drop-down menu. Possible choices are Shell, Perl, Python, Ruby and XML. When done, click *Create Configuration File*.

2.3.3.4   System Details > Configuration > Deploy Files

Under *Deploy Files* you find all files that can be deployed on the selected system. Files from configuration channels with a higher priority take precedence over files from configuration channels with a lower priority.

2.3.3.5   System Details > Configuration > Compare Files

This subtab compares a configuration file stored on the SUSE Manager with the file stored on the client. (It does not compare versions of the same file stored in different channels.) Select the files to be compared, click the *Compare Files* button, select a time to perform the diff, and click the *Schedule Compare* button to confirm. After the diff has been performed, return to this page to see the results.

2.3.3.6   System Details > Configuration > Manage Configuration Channels

This subtab allows you to subscribe to and rank configuration channels associated with the system, lowest first.

The *List/Unsubscribe from Channels* subtab contains a list of the system's configuration channel subscriptions. Click the check box next to the Channel and click *Unsubscribe* to remove the subscription to the channel.

The *Subscribe to Channels* subtab lists all available configuration channels. To subscribe to a channel, select the check box next to it and press *Continue*. To subscribe to all configuration channels, click *Select All* and press *Continue*. The *View/Modify Rankings* page automatically loads.

The *View/Modify Rankings* subtab allows users to set the priority with which files from a particular configuration channel are ranked. The higher the channel is on the list, the more its files take precedence over files on lower-ranked channels. For example, the higher-ranked channel may have an `httpd.conf` file that will take precedence over the same file in a lower-ranked channel.

2.3.4   System Details > Provisioning

The *Provisioning* tab and its subtabs allow you to schedule and monitor AutoYaST or Kickstart installations and to restore a system to its previous state. AutoYaST is a SUSE Linux and Kickstart is a Red Hat utility—both allow you to automate the reinstallation of a system. Snapshot rollbacks provide the ability to revert certain changes on the system. You can roll back a set of RPM packages, but rolling back across multiple update levels is not supported. Both features are described in the sections that follow.

2.3.4.1   System Details > Provisioning > Autoinstallation

This subtab is further divided into *Session Status*, which tracks the progress of previously scheduled autoinstallations, and *Schedule*, which allows you to configure and schedule an autoinstallation for this system.

In the *Schedule* subtab, schedule the selected system for autoinstallation. Choose from the list of available profiles.

 Note

> You must first create a profile before it appears on this subtab.

To alter autoinstallation settings, click on the *Advanced Configuration* button. Configure the network connection and post-installation networking information. You can aggregate multiple network interfaces into a single logical "bonded" interface. In *Kernel Options* specify kernel options to be used during autoinstallation. *Post Kernel Options* are used after the installation is complete and the system is booting for the first time. Configure package profile synchronization.

Select a time for the autoinstallation to begin and click *Schedule Autoinstall and Finish* for all changes to take effect and to schedule the autoinstallation.

Alternatively, click *Create PXE Installation Configuration* to create a Cobbler system record. The selected autoinstallation profile will be used to automatically install the configured distribution next time that particular system boots from PXE. In this case SUSE Manager and its network must be properly configured to allow PXE booting.

 Note

Any settings changed on the *Advanced Configuration* page will be ignored when creating a PXE installation configuration for Cobbler.

The *Variables* subtab can be used to create Kickstart variables, which substitute values in Kickstart files. To define a variable, create a name-value pair (`name/value`) in the text box.

For example, if you want to Kickstart a system that joins the network of a specific organization (for instance the Engineering department) you can create a profile variable to set the IP address and the gateway server address to a variable that any system using that profile will use. Add the following line to the *Variables* text box:

```
IPADDR=192.168.0.28
GATEWAY=192.168.0.1
```

To use the system variable, use the name of the variable in the profile instead of the value. For example, the `network` portion of a Kickstart file could look like the following:

```
network --bootproto=static --device=eth0 --onboot=on --ip=$IPADDR \
  --gateway=$GATEWAY
```

The `$IPADDR` will be `192.168.0.28`, and the `$GATEWAY` will be `192.168.0.1`.

 Note

There is a hierarchy when creating and using variables in Kickstart files. System Kickstart variables take precedence over profile variables, which in turn take precedence over distribution variables. Understanding this hierarchy can alleviate confusion when using variables in Kickstarts.

Using variables are just one part of the larger Cobbler infrastructure for creating templates that can be shared between multiple profiles and systems.

2.3.4.2 System Details > Provisioning > Power Management

SUSE Manager allows you to power on, off, and reboot systems (either physical or bare-metal) via the IPMI protocol if the systems are IPMI-enabled. You need a fully patched SUSE Manager 2.1 installation. To use any power management functionality, IPMI configuration details must be added to SUSE Manager. First select the target system on the systems list, then select *Provisioning* › *Power Management*. On the displayed configuration page, edit all required fields (marked with a red asterisk) and click *Save*.

Systems can be powered on, off, or rebooted from the configuration page via corresponding buttons. Note that any configuration change is also saved in the process. The *Save and Get Status* button can also be used to query for the system's power state. If configuration details are correct, a row is displayed with the current power status ("on" or "off"). If a power management operation succeeds on a system, it will also be noted in its *Event History* tab.

Power management functionalities can also be used from the system set manager to operate on multiple systems at the same time. Specifically, you can change power management configuration parameters or apply operations (power on, off, reboot) to multiple systems at once. In order to do that, add respective systems to the system set manager as described in *Section 2.5, "System Set Manager"*.

Then click on *Manage* › *Provisioning* › *Power Management Configuration* to change one or more configuration parameters for all systems in the set. Note that any field left blank will not alter the configuration parameter in selected systems.

Once all configuration parameters are set correctly, click on *Manage* › *Provisioning* › *Power Management Operations* to power on, off or reboot systems from the set. Note that the Provisioning entitlement is required for non-bare metal systems.

To check that a power operation was executed correctly, click on *System Set Manager* › *Status* on the left-hand menu, then click on the proper line in the list. This will display a new list with systems to which the operation was applied. In the event of errors which prevent correct execution, a brief message with an explanation will be displayed in the *Note* column.

This feature uses Cobbler power management, thus a Cobbler system record is automatically created at first use if it does not exist already. In that case, the automatically created system record will not be bootable from the network and will reference a dummy image. This is needed because Cobbler does not currently support system records without profiles or images. The current implementation of Cobbler power management uses the fence-agent tools to support multiple protocols besides IPMI. Those are not supported by SUSE Manager but can be used by adding the fence agent names as a comma-separated list to the `java.power_management.types` configuration parameter.

2.3.4.3   System Details > Provisioning > Snapshots

Snapshots enable you to roll back the system's package profile, configuration files, and SUSE Manager settings. Snapshots are always captured automatically after an action takes place. The *Snapshots* subtab lists all snapshots for the system, including the reason why the snapshot was taken, the time it was taken, and the number of tags applied to each snapshot.

 Note: Technical Details

- A snapshots is always done *after* a successful operation and not before, as you might expect. One consequence of the fact that snapshots are taken after the action is that, if you want to undo action number X, then you must roll back to the snapshot number X-1.

- It is possible to disable snapshotting globally (in `rhn.conf` set `enable_snapshots = 0`), but it is enabled by default. No further fine tuning is possible.

To revert to a previous configuration, click the *Reason* for the snapshot and review the potential changes on the provided subtabs, starting with *Rollback*.

Important: Unsupported Rollback Scenarios

Snapshot roll backs support the ability to revert *certain* changes to the system, but not in every scenario. For example, you can roll back a set of RPM packages, but rolling back across multiple update levels is not supported.

Rolling back an SP migration is also not supported.

Each subtab provides the specific changes that will be made to the system during the rollback:

- group memberships,

- channel subscriptions,

- installed packages,

- configuration channel subscriptions,

- configuration files,

- snapshot tags.

When satisfied with the reversion, return to the *Rollback* subtab and click the *Rollback to Snapshot* button. To see the list again, click *Return to snapshot list.*

 Note: Background Information About Snapshots

There is no maximum number of snapshots that SUSE Manager will keep, thus related database tables will grow with system count, package count, channel count, and the number of configuration changes over time. Installations with more than a thousand systems should consider setting up a recurring cleanup script via the API or disabling this feature altogether.

There is currently no integrated support for "rotated snapshots".

2.3.4.4   System Details > Provisioning > Snapshot Tags

Snapshot tags provide a means to add meaningful descriptions to your most recent system snapshot. This can be used to indicate milestones, such as a known working configuration or a successful upgrade. To tag the most recent snapshot, click *Create System Tag*, enter a descriptive term in the *Tag name* field, and click the *Tag Current Snapshot* button. You may then revert using this tag directly by clicking its name in the Snapshot Tags list. To delete tags, select their check boxes, click *Remove Tags*, and confirm the action.

2.3.5   System Details > Groups

The *Groups* tab and its subtabs allow you to manage the system's group memberships.

2.3.5.1 System Details > Groups > List/Leave

This subtab lists groups to which the system belongs and enables you to cancel membership. Only System Group Administrators and SUSE Manager Administrators can remove systems from groups. Non-admins just see a *Review this system's group membership* page. To remove the system from one or more groups, select the respective check boxes of these groups and click the *Leave Selected Groups* button. To see the *System Group Details*page, click on the group's name. Refer to *Section 2.4.3, "System Group Details"* for more information.

2.3.5.2 System Details > Groups > Join

Lists groups that the system can be subscribed to. Only System Group Administrators and SUSE Manager Administrators can add a system to groups. Non-admins see a *Review this system's group membership* page. To add the system to groups, select the groups' check boxes and click the *Join Selected Groups* button.

2.3.6 System Details > Audit

Via the *Audit* tab, view OpenSCAP scan results or schedule scans. For more information on auditing and OpenSCAP, refer to *Chapter 6, Audit*.

2.3.7 System Details > Events

Displays past, current, and scheduled actions on the system. You may cancel pending events here. The following sections describe the *Events* subtabs and the features they offer.

2.3.7.1 System Details > Events > Pending

Lists events that are scheduled but have not started. A prerequisite action must complete successfully before the given action is attempted. If an action has a prerequisite, no check box is available to cancel that action. Instead, a check box appears next to the prerequisite action; canceling the prerequisite action causes the action in question to fail.

Actions can be chained so that action 'a' requires action 'b' which requires action 'c'. Action 'c' is performed first and has a check box next to it until it is completed successfully. If any action in the chain fails, the remaining actions also fail. To unschedule a pending event, select the event and click the *Cancel Events* button at the bottom of the page. The following icons indicate the type of events:

- — Package Event,

- — Patch Event,

- — Preferences Event,

- — System Event.

2.3.7.2 System Details > Events > History

The default display of the *Events* tab lists the type and status of events that have failed, occurred or are occurring. To view details of an event, click its summary in the *System History* list. To go back to the table again, click *Return to history list* at the bottom of the page.

2.4 System Groups

The *System Groups* page allows SUSE Manager users to view the *System Groups* list. Only System Group Administrators and SUSE Manager Administrators may perform the following additional tasks:

1. Create system groups. (Refer to *Section 2.4.1, "Creating Groups".*)

2. Add systems to system groups. (Refer to *Section 2.4.2, "Adding and Removing Systems in Groups".*)

3. Remove systems from system groups. (Refer to *Section 2.3, "System Details".*)

4. Assign system group permissions to users. (Refer to *Chapter 9, Users.*)

The *System Groups* list displays all system groups. The list contains several columns for each group:

- *Select* — Via the check boxes add all systems in the selected groups to the *System Set Manager* by clicking the *Update* button. All systems in the selected groups are added to the *System Set Manager*. You can then use the *System Set Manager* to perform actions on them simultaneously. It is possible to select only those systems that are members of all of the selected groups, excluding those systems that belong only to one or some of the selected groups. To do so, select the relevant groups and click the *Work with Intersection* button. To add all systems of all selected groups, click the *Work with Union* button. Each system will show up once, regardless of the number of groups to which it belongs. Refer to *Section 2.5, "System Set Manager"* for details.

- *Updates* — Shows which type of patch alerts are applicable to the group or confirms that all systems are up-to-date. Clicking on a group's status icon takes you to the *Patch* tab of its *System Group Details* page. Refer to *Section 2.4.3, "System Group Details"* for more information. The status icons call for differing degrees of attention:

  - ✓ — All systems in the group are up-to-date.

  - ❗ — Critical patches available, update *strongly* recommended.

  - ⚠ — Updates available and recommended.

- *Health* - Status of the systems in the group, reported by probes.

- *Group Name* — The name of the group as configured during its creation. The name should be explicit enough to distinguish from other groups. Clicking on the name of a group takes you to the *Details* tab of its *System Group Details* page. Refer to *Section 2.4.3, "System Group Details"* for more information.

- *Systems* — Total number of systems in the group. Clicking on the number takes you to the *Systems* tab of the *System Group Details* page for the group. Refer to *Section 2.4.3, "System Group Details"* for more information.

- *Use in SSM* — Clicking the *Use in SSM* link in this column loads all and only the systems in the selected group and launches the *System Set Manager* immediately. Refer to *Section 2.5, "System Set Manager"* for more information.

2.4.1 Creating Groups

To add a new system group, click the *Create Group* link at the top-right corner of the page. Type a name and description and click the *Create Group* button. Make sure you use a name that clearly sets this group apart from others. The new group will appear in the *System Groups* list.

2.4.2 Adding and Removing Systems in Groups

Systems can be added and removed from system groups. Clicking on the group name takes you to the *Details* page. The *Systems* tab shows all systems in the group and allows you to select some or all systems for deletion. Click on *Remove Systems* to remove the selected systems from the group. The *Target Systems* page shows you all systems that can be added to the group. Select the systems and click the *Add Systems* button.

2.4.3 System Group Details

At the top of each *System Group Details* page are two links: *Work With Group* and *Delete Group*. Clicking *Delete Group* deletes the System Group and should be used with caution. Clicking *Work With Group* loads the group's systems and launches the *System Set Manager* immediately just like the *Use Group* button from the *System Groups* list. Refer to *Section 2.5, "System Set Manager"* for more information.

The *System Group Details* page is split into the following tabs:

2.4.3.1 System Group Details > Details

Provides the group name and group description. To change this information, click *Edit These Properties*, make your changes in the appropriate fields, and click the *Update Group* button.

2.4.3.2 System Group Details > Systems

Lists all members of the system group. Clicking links within the table takes you to corresponding tabs within the *System Details* page for the associated system. To remove systems from the group, select the appropriate check boxes and click the *Remove Systems* button on the bottom of the page. Clicking it does not delete systems from SUSE Manager entirely. This is done through the *System Set Manager* or *System Details* pages. Refer to *Section 2.5, "System Set Manager"* or *Section 2.3, "System Details"*, respectively.

2.4.3.3   System Group Details > Target Systems

Target Systems — Lists all systems in your organization. To add systems to the specified system group, click the check boxes to their left and click the *Add Systems* button on the bottom right-hand corner of the page.

2.4.3.4   System Group Details > Patches

List of relevant patches for systems in the system group. Clicking the advisory takes you to the *Details* tab of the *Patch Details* page. (Refer to *Section 4.2.2, "Patch Details"* for more information.) Clicking the Affected Systems number lists all of the systems affected by the patch. To apply the patch updates in this list, select the systems and click the *Apply Patches* button.

2.4.3.5   System Group Details > Admins

List of all organization users that have permission to manage the system group. SUSE Manager Administrators are clearly identified. System Group Administrators are marked with an asterisk (*). To change the system group's users, select and deselect the appropriate check boxes and click the *Update* button.

2.4.3.6   System Group Details > Probes

List of all probes assigned to systems in the system group. *State* shows the status of the probe. Click the individual *System* for details on the probe and to make changes to the probe configuration. Click *Probe* to generate a customizable report on the monitoring.

2.5 *System Set Manager*

The following actions performed for individual systems through the System Details page may be performed for multiple systems via the System Set Manager:

- Apply patch updates.

- Upgrade packages to the most recent versions available.

- Add systems to or remove them from system groups.

- Subscribe/unsubscribe systems to/from channels.

- Update system profiles.

- Modify system preferences such as scheduled download and installation of packages.

- Autoinstall several systems at once.

- Set the subscription and rank of configuration channels.

- Tag the most recent snapshots of your selected systems.

- Revert systems to previous snapshots.

- Run remote commands.

Before performing actions on multiple systems, select the systems you wish to modify. To do so, click the *List the systems* link, check the boxes to the left of the systems you wish to select, and click the *Update List* button.

You can access the System Set Manager in three different ways:

1. Click the *System Set Manager* link in the left navigation area.

2. Click the *Use Group* button in the *System Groups* list.

3. Check the *Work with Group* link on the *System Group Details* page.

2.5.1 System Set Manager > Overview

Description of the various options available to you in the remaining tabs.

2.5.2 System Set Manager > Systems

List of selected systems. To remove systems from this set, select them and click the *Remove* button.

2.5.3 System Set Manager > Patches

List of patch updates applicable to the current system set. Click the number in the Systems column to see to which systems in the System Set Manager a patch applies. To apply updates, select the patches and click the *Apply Patches* button.

2.5.4 System Set Manager > Packages

Click the number in the Systems column to see the systems in the System Set Manager to which a package applies. Modify packages on the system via the following subtabs:

2.5.4.1 System Set Manager > Packages > Install

This list includes all channels to which systems in the set are subscribed. A package is only installed on a system if the system is subscribed to the channel providing the package. Click on the channel name and select the packages from the list. Then click the *Install Packages* button.

2.5.4.2 System Set Manager > Packages > Remove

A list of all the packages installed on the selected systems that might be removed. Multiple versions appear if systems in the System Set Manager have more than one version installed. Select the packages to be deleted, then click the *Remove Packages* button.

2.5.4.3 System Set Manager > Packages > Upgrade

A list of all the packages installed on the selected systems that might be upgraded. Systems must be subscribed to a channel providing the packages to be upgraded. If multiple versions of a package are available, note that your system will be upgraded to the latest version. Select the packages to be upgraded, then click the *Upgrade Packages* button.

2.5.4.4   System Set Manager > Packages > Verify

A list of all installed packages whose contents, file checksum, and other details may be verified. At the next check in, the verify event issues the command `rpm --verify` for the specified package. If there are any discrepancies, they are displayed in the System Details page for each system.

Select the check box next to all packages to be verified, then click the *Verify Packages* button. On the next page, select a date and time for the verification, then click the *Schedule Verifications* button.

2.5.5   System Set Manager > Groups

Tools to create groups and manage membership. These functions are limited to SUSE Manager Administrators and System Group Administrators. To add a new group, click *Create Group* on the top-right corner. In the next page, type the group name and description in the respective fields and click the *Create Group* button. To add or remove selected systems in any of the system groups, toggle the appropriate radio buttons and click the *Alter Membership* button.

2.5.6   System Set Manager > Channels

Manage channel associations through the following subtabs:

2.5.6.1   System Set Manager > Channels > Base Channels

As a Channel Administrator, you may change the base channels your systems are subscribed to. Valid channels are either channels created by your organization, or the vendor's default base channel for your operating system version and processor type. Systems will be unsubscribed from all channels, and subscribed to their new base channels.

 Warning: Changing Base Channel

> This operation can have a dramatic effect on the packages and patches available to the systems. Use with caution.

If you want to change the base channel, select the new one from the *Desired base Channel* and confirm the action.

2.5.6.2 System Set Manager > Channels > Child Channels

To subscribe or unsubscribe selected systems to any of the channels, toggle the appropriate check boxes and click the *Alter Subscriptions* button. Keep in mind that subscribing to a channel uses a channel entitlement for each system in the selected group. If too few entitlements are available, some systems fail to subscribe. Systems must subscribe to a base channel before subscribing to a child channel.

2.5.7 System Set Manager > Configuration

Like in the *System Details > Channels > Configuration* tab, the subtabs here can be used to subscribe the selected systems to configuration channels and deploy and compare the configuration files on the systems. The channels are created in the *Manage Config Channels* interface within the *Channels* category. Refer to *Section 7.2, "Overview"* for channel creation instructions.

To manage the configuration of a system, install the latest `rhncfg*` packages. Refer to *Section 7.1, "Preparing Systems for Config Management"* for instructions on enabling and disabling scheduled actions for a system.

2.5.7.1 System Set Manager > Configuration > Deploy Files

Use this subtab to distribute configuration files from your central repository on SUSE Manager to each of the selected systems. The table lists the configuration files associated with any of the selected systems. Clicking its system count displays the systems already subscribed to the file.

To subscribe the selected systems to the available configuration files, select the check box for each desired file. When done, click *Deploy Configuration* and schedule the action. Note that the latest versions of the files, at the time of scheduling, are deployed. Newer versions created after scheduling are disregarded.

2.5.7.2 System Set Manager > Configuration > Compare Files

Use this subtab to validate configuration files on the selected systems against copies in your central repository on SUSE Manager. The table lists the configuration files associated with any of the selected systems. Clicking a file's system count displays the systems already subscribed to the file.

To compare the configuration files deployed on the systems with those in SUSE Manager, select the check box for each file to be validated. Then click *Analyze Differences* and schedule the action. The comparisons for each system will not complete until each system checks in to SUSE Manager. Once each comparison is complete, any differences between the files will be accessible from each system's events page.

Note that the latest versions of the files, at the time of scheduling, are compared. Newer versions created after scheduling are disregarded. Find the results in the main *Schedule* category or within the *System Details* › *Events* tab.

2.5.7.3   System Set Manager > Configuration > Subscribe to Channels

Subscribe systems to configuration channels according to the order of preference. This tab is available only to SUSE Manager Administrators and Configuration Administrators. Enter a number in the *Rank* column to subscribe to a channel. Channels are accessed in the order of their rank, starting with the number 1. Channels not assigned a numeric value are not associated with the selected systems. Your local configuration channel always overrides all other channels. Once you have established the rank of the config channels, you must decide how they are applied to the selected systems.

The three buttons below the channels reflect your options. Clicking *Subscribe with Highest Priority* places all the ranked channels before any other channels to which the selected systems are currently subscribed. Clicking *Subscribe With Lowest Priority* places the ranked channels after those channels to which the selected systems are currently subscribed. Clicking *Replace Existing Subscriptions* removes any existing association and creates new ones with the ranked channels, leaving every system with the same config channels in the same order.

In the first two cases, if any of the newly ranked config channels are already in a system's existing config channel list, the duplicate channel is removed and replaced according to the new rank, effectively reordering the system's existing channels. When such conflicts exist, you are presented with a confirmation page to ensure the intended action is correct. When the change has taken place, a message appears at the top of the page indicating the update was successful.

2.5.7.4 System Set Manager > Configuration > Unsubscribe from Channels

Administrators may unsubscribe systems from configuration channels by clicking the check box next to the channel name and clicking the *Unsubscribe Systems* button.

2.5.7.5 System Set Manager > Configuration > Enable Configuration

Administrators may enable configuration channel management by clicking the check box next to the channel name and clicking the *Enable Configuration Management* button. You can also schedule the action by clicking the *Schedule package installs for no sooner than* radio button and using the drop-down menus to configure date and time, then clicking *Enable Configuration Management*.

2.5.8 System Set Manager > Provisioning

Set the options for provisioning systems via the following subtabs.

2.5.8.1 System Set Manager > Provisioning > Autoinstallation

Use this subtab to reinstall a client. To schedule autoinstallations for these systems, select a distribution. The autoinstallation profile used for each system in the set is determined via the *Autoinstallable Type* radio buttons.

Choose *Select autoinstallation profile* if you want to apply the same profile to all systems in the set. This is the default option. You will see a list of available profiles to select from once you click on *Continue*.

Choose *Autoinstall by IP Address* if you want to apply different autoinstallation profiles to different systems in the set, by IP address. To do so, at least two autoinstallation profiles must be configured with associated IP ranges.

If you use *Autoinstall by IP Address*, SUSE Manager will automatically pick a profile for each system so that the system's IP address will be in one of the IP ranges specified in the profile itself. If such a profile cannot be found, SUSE Manager will look for an organization default profile and apply that instead. If no matching IP ranges nor organization default profiles can be found, no autoinstallation will be performed on the system. You will be notified on the next page if that happens.

To use Cobbler system records for autoinstallation, select *Create PXE Installation Configuration*. With PXE boot, you can not only reinstall clients, but automatically install machines that don't have an operating system installed yet. SUSE Manager and its network must be properly configured to enable PXE booting.

 Note

> If a system set contains bare-metal systems and installed clients, only features working for systems without an operating system installed will be available. Full features will be enabled again once all bare-metal systems are removed from the set.

If any of the systems connect to SUSE Manager via a proxy server, choose either the *Preserve Existing Configuration* radio button or the *Use Proxy* radio button. If you choose to autoinstall through a proxy server, select from the available proxies listed in the drop-down box beside the *Use Proxy* radio button. All of the selected systems will autoinstall via the selected proxy. Click the *Schedule Autoinstall* button to confirm your selections. When the autoinstallations for the selected systems are successfully scheduled, you will return to the *System Set Manager* page.

2.5.8.2   System Set Manager > Provisioning > Tag Systems

Use this subtab to add meaningful descriptions to the most recent snapshots of your selected systems. To tag the most recent system snapshots, enter a descriptive term in the *Tag name* field and click the *Tag Current Snapshots* button.

2.5.8.3   System Set Manager > Provisioning > Rollback

Use this subtab to rollback selected Provisioning-entitled systems to previous snapshots marked with a tag. Click the tag name, verify the systems to be reverted, and click the *Rollback Systems* button.

2.5.8.4　System Set Manager > Provisioning > Remote Command

Use this subtab to issue remote commands on selected Provisioning-entitled systems. First create a `run` file on the client systems to allow this function to operate. Refer to *Section 2.3.1.3, " System Details > Details > Remote Command "* for instructions. Then identify a specific user, group, timeout period, and the script to run. Select a date and time to execute the command and click *Schedule*.

2.5.8.5　System Set Manager > Provisioning > Power Management Configuration

2.5.8.6　System Set Manager > Provisioning > Power Management Operation

2.5.9　System Set Manager > Audit

System sets can be scheduled for XCCDF scans. Enter the command and command-line arguments, as well as the path to the XCCDF document. Then schedule the scan. All target systems are listed below with a flag whether they support OpenSCAP scans. For more details on OpenSCAP and audits, refer to *Chapter 6, Audit*.

2.5.10　System Set Manager > Misc

On the *Misc* page, you can modify *Custom System Information*. Click *Set a custom value for selected systems*, then the name of a key. Enter values for all selected systems, then click the *Set Values* button. To remove values for all selected systems, click *Remove a custom value from selected systems*, then the name of the key. Click the *Remove Values* button to delete.

Set *System Preferences* via the respective radio buttons.

2.5.10.1　System Set Manager > Misc > Hardware

Click on the *Hardware* subtab to schedule a hardware profile refresh. Click *Confirm Refresh*.

2.5.10.2   System Set Manager > Misc > Software

Click the *Software* subtab, then the *Confirm Refresh* button to schedule a package profile update of the selected systems.

2.5.10.3   System Set Manager > Misc > Migrate

Click the *Migrate* subtab to move selected systems to a selected organization.

2.5.10.4   System Set Manager > Misc > Lock/Unlock

Select the *Lock/Unlock* subtab to select systems to be excluded from package updates. Enter a *Lock reason* in the text field and click the *Lock* button. Already locked systems can be unlocked on this page. Select them and click *Unlock*.

2.5.10.5   System Set Manager > Misc > Reboot

Select the appropriate systems, then click the *Reboot Systems* link to select these systems for reboot. To cancel this action, click the *list of systems* link that appears within the confirmation message at the top of the page, select the systems, and click *Unschedule Action*.

2.5.10.6   System Set Manager > Misc > Delete

Click the *Delete* subtab, to remove systems by deleting their system profiles. Click the *Confirm Deletions* button to remove the selected profiles permanently.

2.6 Advanced Search

Carry out a *System Search* on your systems according to the following criteria: system details, hardware, devices, interface, networking, packages, and location.

Refine searches using the *Fields to Search* drop-down menu, which is set to *Name/Description* by default.

The Activity selections (*Days Since Last Check-in*, for instance) are useful in finding and removing outdated system profiles.

Type the keyword, select the criterion to search by, use the radio buttons to specify whether you wish to query all systems or only those in the *System Set Manager,* and click the *Search* button. To list all systems that do *not* match the criteria, select the *Invert Result* check box.

The results appear at the bottom of the page. For details on how to use the resulting system list, refer to *Section 2.2, "Systems".*

2.7 Activation Keys

Users with the Activation Key Administrator role (including SUSE Manager Administrators) can generate activation keys in the SUSE Manager Web interface. With such an activation key, register a SUSE Linux Enterprise or Red Hat Enterprise Linux system, entitle the system to a SUSE Manager service level and subscribe the system to specific channels and system groups through the `rhnreg_ks` command line utility.

 Note

System-specific activation keys created through the *Reactivation* subtab of the *System Details* page are not part of this list because they are not reusable across systems.

For more information about Activation Keys, see *Book "SUSE Manager Best Practices", Chapter 5 "Activation Key Management".*

2.7.1 Managing Activation Keys

To create an activation key:

PROCEDURE 2.1: CREATING ACTIVATION KEYS

1. Select *Systems* from the top navigation bar then *Activation Keys* from the left navigation bar.

2. Click the *Create Key* link at the upper right corner.

3. *Description* — Enter a *Description* to identify the generated activation key.

4. *Key* — Either choose automatic generation by leaving this field blank or enter the key you want to generate in the *Key* field. This string of characters can then be used with `rhnreg_ks` to register client systems with SUSE Manager. Refer to *Section 2.7.2, "Using Multiple Activation Keys at Once"* for details.

 Warning: Allowed Characters

Do not insert commas or double quotes in the key. All other characters are allowed, but `<> (){}` (this includes the space) will get removed automatically. If the string is empty, a random one is generated.

Commas are problematic because they are used as separator when two or more activation keys are used at once.

5. *Usage* — The maximum number systems that can be registered with the activation key concurrently. Leave blank for unlimited use. Deleting a system profile reduces the usage count by one and registering a system profile with the key increases the usage count by one.

6. *Base Channels* — The primary channel for the key. This can be either the `SUSE Manager Default` channel, a SUSE provided channel, or a custom base channel.
Selecting `SUSE Manager Default` allows client systems to register with the SUSE-provided default channel that corresponds with their installed version of SUSE Linux Enterprise. You can also associate the key with a custom base channel. If a system using this key is not compatible with the selected channel, it will fall back to the SUSE Manager default channel.

7. *Add-on System Types* — The supplemental system types for the key, e. g. Virtualization Host. All systems will receive these system types with the key.

8. *Contact Method* - Select how clients communicate with SUSE Manager. *Pull* waits for the client to check in. With *Push via SSH* and *Push via SSH tunnel* the server contacts the client via SSH (with or without tunnel) and pushes updates and actions, etc.
For more information about contact methods, see *Book "SUSE Manager Best Practices", Chapter 6 "Contact Methods"*.

9. *Universal Default* — Select whether or not this key should be considered the primary activation key for your organization.

Warning: Changing the Default Activation Key

Only one universal default activation key can be defined per organization. If a universal key already exists for this organization, you will unset the currently used universal key by activating the check box.

10. Click *Create Activation Key*.

To create more activation keys, repeat the steps above.

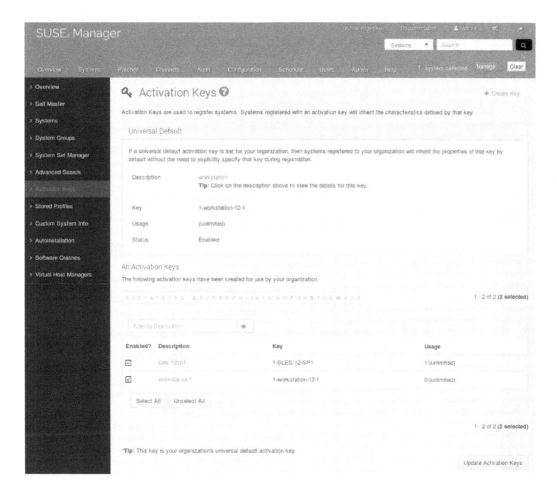

FIGURE 2.1: ACTIVATION KEYS

After creating the unique key, it appears in the list of activation keys along with the number of times it has been used (see *Figure 2.1, "Activation Keys"*). Only Activation Key Administrators can see this list. At this point, you can configure the key further, for example, associate the key with child channels (e.g., the Tools child channel), packages (e.g., the `rhncfg-actions` package) and groups. Systems registered with the key get automatically subscribed to them.

To change the settings of a key, click the key's description in the list to display its *Details* page (see *Figure 2.2, "Activation Key Details With Subtabs"*). Via additional tabs you can select child channels, packages, configuration channels, group membership and view activated systems. Modify the appropriate tab then click the *Update Activation Key* button. To disassociate channels and groups from a key, deselect them in the respective menus by `Ctrl`-clicking their highlighted names. To remove a key entirely, click the *Delete Key* link in the upper right corner of the *Details* page. In the upper right corner find also the *Clone Key* link.

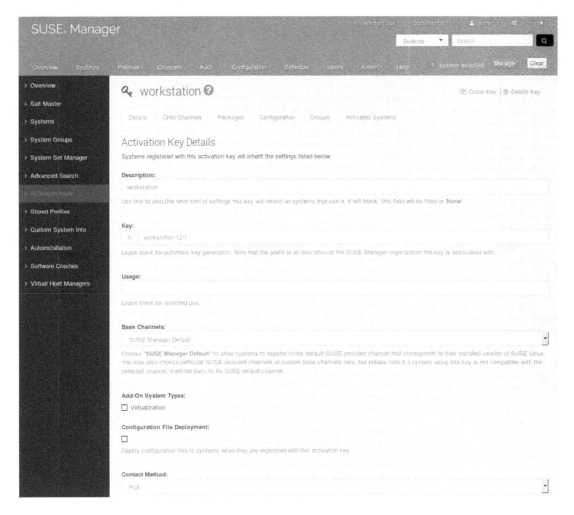

FIGURE 2.2: ACTIVATION KEY DETAILS WITH SUBTABS

Any (client tools) package installation requires that the Client Tools channel is available and the *Provisioning* checkbox is selected. The Client Tools channel should be selected in the *Child Channels* tab.

After you created the activation key, you can see in the *Details* tab a checkbox named *Configuration File Deployment*. If you select it, all needed packages are automatically added to the *Packages* list. By default, the following packages are added: `rhncfg`, `rhncfg-client`, and `rhncfg-actions`.

If you select *Virtualization Host* you automatically get the following package: `rhn-virtualization-host`.

Adding the `osad` packages makes sense if you want to execute scheduled actions immediately after the schedule time.

A system may be subscribed to a base channel during registration with an activation key. However, if the activation key specifies a base channel that is not compatible with the operating system running on the system, the registration fails. For example, a SUSE Linux Enterprise Server for x86 system cannot register with an Activation Key that specifies a SUSE Linux Enterprise Server for x86_64 base channel. A system can always subscribe to a custom base channel.

To disable system activations with a key, uncheck the corresponding box in the *Enabled* column in the key list. The key can be re-enabled by selecting the check box. Click the *Update Activation Keys* button on the bottom right-hand corner of the page to activate your changes.

2.7.2 Using Multiple Activation Keys at Once

Multiple activation keys can be specified at the command-line or in a single autoinstallation profile. This allows you to aggregate the aspects of various keys without recreating a specific key for every system that you want to register, simplifying the registration and autoinstallation processes while slowing the growth of your key list.

Without this stacking ability, your organization would need at least six activation keys to manage four server groups and subscribe a server to any two groups. Factor in two versions of the operating system and you need twice the number of activation keys. A larger organization would need keys in the dozens.

Registering with multiple activation keys requires some caution; conflicts between some values cause registration to fail. Conflicts in the following values do not cause registration to fail, a combination of values is applied: software packages, software child channels, and configuration channels. Conflicts in the remaining properties are resolved in the following manner:

- Base software channels: registration fails.

- System types: registration fails.

- Enable configuration flag: configuration management is set.

Do not use system-specific activation keys along with other activation keys; registration fails in this event.

You are now ready to use multiple activation keys at once. Separate keys with a comma at the command line with `rhnreg_ks` or in a Kickstart profile in the *Activation Keys* tab of the *Autoinstallation Details* page.

2.8 Stored Profiles

SUSE Manager Provisioning customers can create package profiles via the *System Details* page. Under *Software › Packages › Profiles*, click on *Create System Profile*. Enter a *Profile Name* and *Profile Description*, then click *Create Profile*. These profiles are displayed on the *Stored Profiles* page (left navigation bar), where they can be edited or deleted.

To edit a profile, click its name in the list, alter its name or description, and click the *Update* button. To view software associated with the profile, click the *Packages* subtab. To remove the profile entirely, click *Delete Profile* at the upper-right corner of the page.

2.9 Custom System Info

SUSE Manager customers may include completely customizable information about their systems. Unlike with notes, the information here is more formal and can be searched. For instance, you may decide to specify an asset tag for each system. To do so, select *Custom System Info* from the left navigation bar and create an `asset` key.

Click *Create Key* in the upper-right corner of the page. Enter a suitable label and description, such as `Asset` and `Precise location of each system`, then click *Create Key*. The key will show up in the custom info keys list.

Once the key exists, you may assign a value to it through the *Custom Info* tab of the *System Details* page. Refer to *Section 2.3.1.8, " System Details > Details > Custom Info "* for instructions.

2.10 Autoinstallation

 Note: Autoinstallation Types: AutoYaST and Kickstart

In the following section, AutoYaST and AutoYaST features apply for SUSE Linux Enterprise client systems only. For RHEL systems, use Kickstart and Kickstart features.

AutoYaST and Kickstart configuration files allow administrators to create an environment for automating otherwise time-consuming system installations, such as multiple servers or workstations. AutoYaST files have to be uploaded to be managed with SUSE Manager. Kickstart files can be created, modified, and managed within the SUSE Manager Web interface.

SUSE Manager also features the Cobbler installation server.

SUSE Manager provides an interface for developing Kickstart and AutoYaST profiles that can be used to install Red Hat Enterprise Linux or SUSE Linux Enterprise on either new or already-registered systems automatically according to certain specifications.

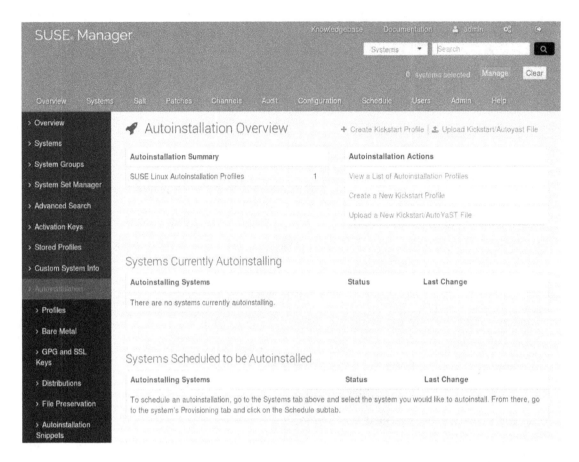

FIGURE 2.3: AUTOINSTALLATION OVERVIEW

This overview page displays the status of automated installations (Kickstart and AutoYaST) on your client systems: the types and number of profiles you have created and the progress of systems that are scheduled to be installed using Kickstart or AutoYaST. In the upper right is the *Autoinstallation Actions* section, which contains a series of links to management actions for your Kickstart or AutoYaST profiles. Before explaining the various automated installation options on this page, the next two sections provide an introduction to AutoYaST (*Section 2.10.1, "Introduction to AutoYaST"*) and **Kickstart** (*Section 2.10.2, "Introduction to Kickstart"*).

2.10.1 Introduction to AutoYaST

Using AutoYaST, a system administrator can create a single file containing the answers to all the questions that would normally be asked during a typical installation of a SUSE Linux Enterprise system.

AutoYaST files can be kept on a single server system and read by individual computers during the installation. This way the same AutoYaST file is used to install SUSE Linux Enterprise on multiple machines.

The *SUSE Linux Enterprise Server Deployment Guide* (http://www.suse.com/documentation/sles-12/book_sle_deployment/data/cha_deployment_autoinst.html) **contains an** in-depth discussion of "Automated Installation" using AutoYaST.

2.10.1.1 AutoYaST Explained

When a machine is to receive a network-based AutoYaST installation, the following events must occur in this order:

1. After being connected to the network and turned on, the machine's PXE logic broadcasts its MAC address and requests to be discovered.

2. If no static IP address is used, the DHCP server recognizes the discovery request and offers network information needed for the new machine to boot. This includes an IP address, the default gateway to be used, the netmask of the network, the IP address of the TFTP or HTTP server holding the bootloader program, and the full path and file name to that program (relative to the server's root).

3. The machine applies the networking information and initiates a session with the server to request the bootloader program.

4. The bootloader searches for its configuration file on the server from which it was loaded. This file dictates which Kernel and Kernel options, such as the initial RAM disk (initrd) image, should be executed on the booting machine. Assuming the bootloader program is SYSLINUX, this file is located in the `pxelinux.cfg` directory on the server and named the hexadecimal equivalent of the new machine's IP address. For example, a bootloader configuration file for SUSE Linux Enterprise Server should contain:

```
port 0
prompt 0
timeout 1
default autoyast
label autoyast
  kernel vmlinuz
```

```
append autoyast=http://my_susemanager_server/path \
  install=http://my_susemanager_server/repo_tree
```

5. The machine accepts and uncompresses the initrd and kernel, boots the kernel, fetches the instsys from the install server and initiates the AutoYaST installation with the options supplied in the bootloader configuration file, including the server containing the AutoYaST configuration file.

6. The new machine is installed based on the parameters established within the AutoYaST configuration file.

2.10.1.2   AutoYaST Prerequisites

Some preparation is required for your infrastructure to handle AutoYaST installations. For instance, before creating AutoYaST profiles, you may consider:

- A DHCP server is not required for AutoYaST, but it can make things easier. If you are using static IP addresses, you should select static IP while developing your AutoYaST profile.

- Host the AutoYaST distribution trees via HTTP, properly provided by SUSE Manager.

- If conducting a so-called bare-metal AutoYaST installation, you should do the following:

  - Configure DHCP to assign the required networking parameters and the bootloader program location.

  - In the bootloader configuration file, specify the kernel and appropriate kernel options to be used.

2.10.1.3   Building Bootable AutoYaST ISOs

While you can schedule a registered system to be installed by AutoYaST with a new operating system and package profile, you can also automatically install a system that is not registered with SUSE Manager, or does not yet have an operating system installed. One common method of doing this is to create a bootable CD-ROM that is inserted into the target system. When the system is rebooted or switched on, it boots from the CD-ROM, loads the AutoYaST configuration from your SUSE Manager, and proceeds to install SUSE Linux Enterprise Server according to the AutoYaST profile you have created.

To use the CD-ROM, boot the system and type `autoyast` at the prompt (assuming you left the label for the AutoYaST boot as `autoyast`). When you press `Enter`, the AutoYaST installation begins.

For more information about image creation, refer to the *SUSE Linux Enterprise Server Deployment Guide*, Part "Imaging and Creating Products".

2.10.1.4   Integrating AutoYaST with PXE

In addition to CD-ROM-based installations, AutoYaST installation through a Pre-Boot Execution Environment (PXE) is supported. This is less error-prone than CDs, enables AutoYaST installation from bare metal, and integrates with existing PXE/DHCP environments.

To use this method, make sure your systems have network interface cards (NIC) that support PXE, install and configure a PXE server, ensure DHCP is running, and place the installation repository on an HTTP server for deployment. Finally upload the AutoYaST profile via the Web interface to the SUSE Manager server. Once the AutoYaST profile has been created, use the URL from the *Autoinstallation Overview* page, as for CD-ROM-based installations.

To obtain specific instructions for conducting PXE AutoYaST installation, refer to the *Using PXE Boot* section of the *SUSE Linux Enterprise Deployment Guide*.

Starting with *Section 2.10.3, "Autoinstallation > Profiles (Kickstart and AutoYaST)"*, AutoYaST options available from *Systems › Kickstart* are described.

2.10.2   Introduction to Kickstart

Using Kickstart, a system administrator can create a single file containing the answers to all the questions that would normally be asked during a typical installation of Red Hat Enterprise Linux.

Kickstart files can be kept on a single server and read by individual computers during the installation. This method allows you to use one Kickstart file to install Red Hat Enterprise Linux on multiple machines.

The *Red Hat Enterprise Linux System Administration Guide* contains an in-depth description of Kickstart (https://access.redhat.com/documentation/en/red-hat-enterprise-linux/).

2.10.2.1 Kickstart Explained

When a machine is to receive a network-based Kickstart, the following events must occur in this order:

1. After being connected to the network and turned on, the machine's PXE logic broadcasts its MAC address and requests to be discovered.

2. If no static IP address is used, the DHCP server recognizes the discovery request and offers network information needed for the new machine to boot. This information includes an IP address, the default gateway to be used, the netmask of the network, the IP address of the TFTP or HTTP server holding the bootloader program, and the full path and file name of that program (relative to the server's root).

3. The machine applies the networking information and initiates a session with the server to request the bootloader program.

4. The bootloader searches for its configuration file on the server from which it was loaded. This file dictates which kernel and kernel options, such as the initial RAM disk (initrd) image, should be executed on the booting machine. Assuming the bootloader program is SYSLINUX, this file is located in the `pxelinux.cfg` directory on the server and named the hexadecimal equivalent of the new machine's IP address. For example, a bootloader configuration file for Red Hat Enterprise Linux AS 2.1 should contain:

```
port 0
prompt 0
timeout 1
default My_Label
label My_Label
        kernel vmlinuz
        append ks=http://my_susemanager_server/path \
            initrd=initrd.img network apic
```

5. The machine accepts and uncompresses the init image and kernel, boots the kernel, and initiates a Kickstart installation with the options supplied in the bootloader configuration file, including the server containing the Kickstart configuration file.

6. This Kickstart configuration file in turn directs the machine to the location of the installation files.

7. The new machine is built based on the parameters established within the Kickstart configuration file.

2.10.2.2 Kickstart Prerequisites

Some preparation is required for your infrastructure to handle Kickstarts. For instance, before creating Kickstart profiles, you may consider:

* A DHCP server is not required for kickstarting, but it can make things easier. If you are using static IP addresses, select static IP while developing your Kickstart profile.

* An FTP server can be used instead of hosting the Kickstart distribution trees via HTTP.

* If conducting a bare metal Kickstart, you should configure DHCP to assign required networking parameters and the bootloader program location. Also, specify within the bootloader configuration file the kernel to be used and appropriate kernel options.

2.10.2.3 Building Bootable Kickstart ISOs

While you can schedule a registered system to be kickstarted to a new operating system and package profile, you can also Kickstart a system that is not registered with SUSE Manager or does not yet have an operating system installed. One common method of doing this is to create a bootable CD-ROM that is inserted into the target system. When the system is rebooted, it boots from the CD-ROM, loads the Kickstart configuration from your SUSE Manager, and proceeds to install Red Hat Enterprise Linux according to the Kickstart profile you have created.

To do this, copy the contents of `/isolinux` from the first CD-ROM of the target distribution. Then edit the `isolinux.cfg` file to default to 'ks'. Change the 'ks' section to the following template:

```
label ks
kernel vmlinuz
  append text ks=url initrd=initrd.img lang= devfs=nomount \
    ramdisk_size=16438 ksdevice
```

IP address-based Kickstart URLs will look like this:

```
http://my.manager.server/kickstart/ks/mode/ip_range
```

The Kickstart distribution defined via the IP range should match the distribution from which you are building, or errors will occur. *ksdevice* is optional, but looks like:

```
ksdevice=eth0
```

It is possible to change the distribution for a Kickstart profile within a family, such as Red Hat Enterprise Linux AS 4 to Red Hat Enterprise Linux ES 4, by specifying the new distribution label. Note that you cannot move between versions (4 to 5) or between updates (U1 to U2).

Next, customize `isolinux.cfg` further for your needs by adding multiple Kickstart options, different boot messages, shorter timeout periods, etc.

Next, create the ISO as described in the *Making an Installation Boot CD-ROM* section of the *Red Hat Enterprise Linux Installation Guide*. Alternatively, issue the command:

```
mkisofs -o file.iso -b isolinux.bin -c boot.cat -no-emul-boot \
  -boot-load-size 4 -boot-info-table -R -J -v -T isolinux/
```

Note that `isolinux/` is the relative path to the directory containing the modified isolinux files copied from the distribution CD, while `file.iso` is the output ISO file, which is placed into the current directory.

Burn the ISO to CD-ROM and insert the disc. Boot the system and type "ks" at the prompt (assuming you left the label for the Kickstart boot as 'ks'). When you press `Enter`, Kickstart starts running.

2.10.2.4   Integrating Kickstart with PXE

In addition to CD-ROM-based installs, Kickstart supports a Pre-Boot Execution Environment (PXE). This is less error-prone than CDs, enables kickstarting from bare metal, and integrates with existing PXE/DHCP environments.

To use this method, make sure your systems have network interface cards (NIC) that support PXE. Install and configure a PXE server and ensure DHCP is running. Then place the appropriate files on an HTTP server for deployment. Once the Kickstart profile has been created, use the URL from the *Kickstart Details* page, as for CD-ROM-based installs.

To obtain specific instructions for conducting PXE Kickstarts, refer to the *PXE Network Installations* chapter of the *Red Hat Enterprise Linux 4 System Administration Guide*.

 Note: Tip

Running the Network Booting Tool, as described in the Red Hat Enterprise Linux 4: System Administration Guide, select "HTTP" as the protocol and include the domain name of the SUSE Manager in the Server field if you intend to use it to distribute the installation files.

The following sections describe the autoinstallation options available from the *Systems > Autoinstallation* page.

2.10.3 Autoinstallation > Profiles (Kickstart and AutoYaST)

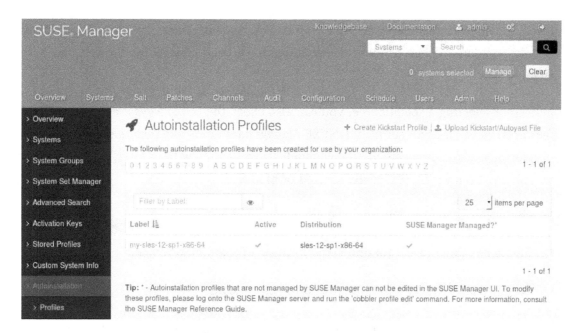

FIGURE 2.4: AUTOINSTALLATION PROFILES

This page lists all profiles for your organization, shows whether these profiles are active, and specifies the distribution tree with which each profile is associated. You can either create a new Kickstart profile by clicking the *Create Kickstart Profile* link, upload or paste the contents of a new profile using the *Upload Kickstart/Autoyast File*, or edit an existing Kickstart profile by clicking the name of the profile. Note, you can only update AutoYaST profiles using the upload button. You can also view AutoYaST profiles in the edit box or change the virtualization type using the selection list.

2.10.3.1   Create a New Kickstart Profile

Click on the *Create Kickstart Profile* link from the *Systems › Autoinstallation* page to start the wizard that populates the base values needed for a Kickstart profile.

PROCEDURE 2.2: CREATING A KICKSTART PROFILE

1. On the first line, enter a Kickstart profile label. This label cannot contain spaces, so use dashes (-) or underscores (_) as separators.

2. Select a *Base Channel* for this profile, which consists of packages based on a specific architecture and Red Hat Enterprise Linux release.

3. Select an *Autoinstallable Tree* for this profile. The *Autoinstallable Tree* drop-down menu is only populated if one or more distributions have been created for the selected base channel (see *Section 2.10.6, " Autoinstallation > Distributions "*).

4. Instead of selecting a specific tree, you can also check the box *Always use the newest Tree for this base channel.* This setting lets SUSE Manager automatically pick the latest tree that is associated with the specified base channels. If you add new trees later, SUSE Manager will always keep the most recently created or modified.

5. Select the *Virtualization Type* from the drop-down menu.

6. On the second page, select (or enter) the location of the Kickstart tree.

7. On the third page, select a root password for the system.

Depending on your base channel, your newly created Kickstart profile might be subscribed to a channel that is missing required packages. For Kickstart to work properly, the following packages should be present in its base channel: `pyOpenSSL`, `rhnlib`, `libxml2-python`, and `spacewalk-koan` and associated packages.

To resolve this issue:

- Make sure that the Tools software channel for the Kickstart profile's base channel is available to your organization. If it is not, you must request entitlements for the Tools software channel from the SUSE Manager administrator.

- Make sure that the Tools software channel for this Kickstart profile's base channel is available to your SUSE Manager as a child channel.

- Make sure that `rhn-kickstart` and associated packages corresponding to this Kickstart are available in the Tools child channel.

The final stage of the wizard presents the *Autoinstallation Details > Details* tab. On this tab and the other subtabs, nearly every option for the new Kickstart profile can be customized.

Once created, you can access the Kickstart profile by downloading it from the *Autoinstallation Details* page by clicking the *Autoinstallation File* subtab and clicking the *Download Autoinstallation File* link.

If the Kickstart file is *not* managed by SUSE Manager, you can access it via the following URL:

```
http://my.manager.server/ks/dist/ks-rhel-ARCH-VARIANT-VERSION
```

In the above example, `ARCH` is the architecture of the Kickstart file, `VARIANT` is either `client` or `server`, and `VERSION` is the release of Red Hat Enterprise Linux associated with the Kickstart file.

The following sections describe the options available on each subtab.

2.10.3.1.1 Autoinstallation Details > Details

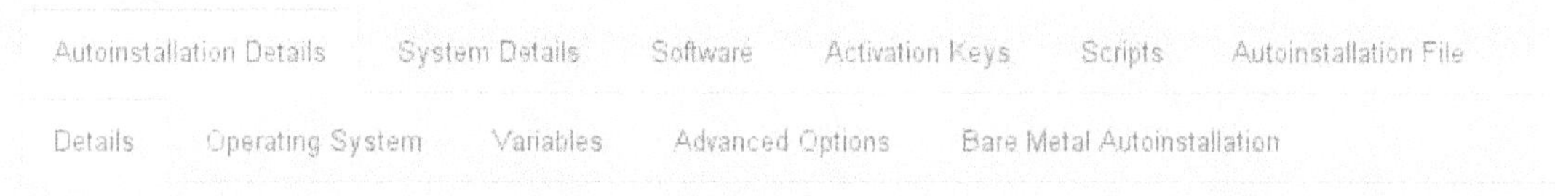

Autoinstallation Details	System Details	Software	Activation Keys	Scripts	Autoinstallation File
Details	Operating System	Variables	Advanced Options	Bare Metal Autoinstallation	

FIGURE 2.5: AUTOINSTALLATION DETAILS

Figure 2.5, "Autoinstallation Details" shows the subtabs that are available. On the *Autoinstallation Details > Details* page, you have the following options:

- Change the profile *Label*.

- Change the operating system by clicking on *(Change)*.

- Change the *Virtualization Type.*

 Note

> Changing the *Virtualization Type* may require changes to the Kickstart profile bootloader and partition options, potentially overwriting user customizations. Consult the *Partitioning* tab to verify any new or changed settings.

- Change the amount of *Virtual Memory* (in Megabytes of RAM) allocated to virtual guests autoinstalled with this profile.

- Change the number of *Virtual CPUs* for each virtual guest.

- Change the *Virtual Storage Path* from the default in `/var/lib/xen/`.

- Change the amount of *Virtual Disk Space* (in GB) allotted to each virtual guest.

- Change the *Virtual Bridge* for networking of the virtual guest.

- Deactivate the profile so that it cannot be used to schedule a Kickstart by removing the *Active* check mark.

- Check whether to enable logging for custom `%post` scripts to the `/root/ks-post.log` file.

- Decide whether to enable logging for custom `%pre` scripts to the `/root/ks-pre.log` file.

- Choose whether to preserve the `ks.cfg` file and all `%include` fragments to the `/root/` directory of all systems autoinstalled with this profile.

- Select whether this profile is the default for all of your organization's Kickstarts by checking or unchecking the box.

- Add any *Kernel Options* in the corresponding text box.

- Add any *Post Kernel Options* in the corresponding text box.

- Enter comments that are useful to you in distinguishing this profile from others.

2.10.3.1.2 Autoinstallation Details > Operating System

On this page, you can make the following changes to the operating system that the Kickstart profile installs:

Change the base channel

Select from the available base channels. SUSE Manager administrators see a list of all base channels that are currently synced to the SUSE Manager.

Child Channels

Subscribe to available child channels of the base channel, such as the Tools channel.

Available Trees

Use the drop-down menu to choose from available trees associated with the base channel.

Always use the newest Tree for this base channel.

Instead of selecting a specific tree, you can also check the box *Always use the newest Tree for this base channel.* This setting lets SUSE Manager automatically pick the latest tree that is associated with the specified base channels. If you add new trees later, SUSE Manager will always keep the most recently created or modified.

Software URL (File Location)

The exact location from which the Kickstart tree is mounted. This value is determined when the profile is created. You can view it on this page but you cannot change it.

2.10.3.1.3 Autoinstallation Details > Variables

Autoinstallation variables can substitute values in Kickstart and AutoYaST profiles. To define a variable, create a name-value pair (*name/value*) in the text box.

For example, if you want to autoinstall a system that joins the network of a specified organization (for example the Engineering department), you can create a profile variable to set the IP address and the gateway server address to a variable that any system using that profile will use. Add the following line to the *Variables* text box.

```
IPADDR=192.168.0.28
GATEWAY=192.168.0.1
```

Now you can use the name of the variable in the profile instead of a specific value. For example, the `network` part of a Kickstart file looks like the following:

```
network --bootproto=static --device=eth0 --onboot=on --ip=$IPADDR \
  --gateway=$GATEWAY
```

The `$IPADDR` will be resolved to `192.168.0.28`, and the `$GATEWAY` to `192.168.0.1`

 Note

There is a hierarchy when creating and using variables in Kickstart files. System Kickstart variables take precedence over *Profile* variables, which in turn take precedence over *Distribution* variables. Understanding this hierarchy can alleviate confusion when using variables in Kickstarts.

Using variables are just one part of the larger Cobbler infrastructure for creating templates that can be shared between multiple profiles and systems.

2.10.3.1.4   Autoinstallation Details > Advanced Options

From this page, you can toggle several installation options on and off by checking and unchecking the boxes to the left of the option. For most installations, the default options are correct. Refer to Red Hat Enterprise Linux documentation for details.

2.10.3.1.5   Assigning Default Profiles to an Organization

You can specify an Organization Default Profile by clicking on *Autoinstallation > Profiles > profile name > Details,* then checking the *Organization Default Profile* box and finally clicking on *Update*.

2.10.3.1.6   Assigning IP Ranges to Profiles

You can associate an IP range to an autoinstallation profile by clicking on *Autoinstallation > Profiles > profile name > Bare Metal Autoinstallation,* adding an IPv4 range and finally clicking on *Add IP Range*.

2.10.3.1.7   Autoinstallation Details > Bare Metal Autoinstallation

This subtab provides the information necessary to Kickstart systems that are not currently registered with SUSE Manager. Using the on-screen instructions, you may either autoinstall systems using boot media (CD-ROM) or by IP address.

2.10.3.1.8   System Details > Details

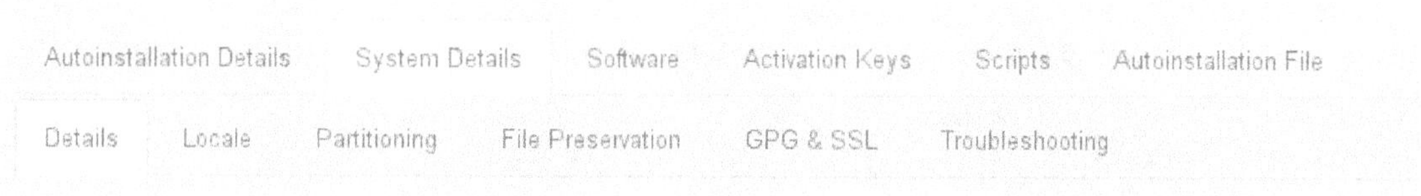

Autoinstallation Details   System Details   Software   Activation Keys   Scripts   Autoinstallation File

Details   Locale   Partitioning   File Preservation   GPG & SSL   Troubleshooting

FIGURE 2.6: SYSTEM DETAILS

Figure 2.6, "System Details" shows the subtabs that are available from the *System Details* tab. On the *System Details › Details* page, you have the following options:

- Select between DHCP and static IP, depending on your network.

- Choose the level of SELinux that is configured on kickstarted systems.

- Enable configuration management or remote command execution on kickstarted systems.

- Change the root password associated with this profile.

2.10.3.1.9   System Details > Locale

Change the timezone for kickstarted systems.

2.10.3.1.10   System Details > Partitioning

From this subtab, indicate the partitions that you wish to create during installation. For example:

```
partition /boot --fstype=ext3 --size=200
partition swap --size=2000
partition pv.01 --size=1000 --grow
volgroup myvg pv.01 logvol / --vgname=myvg --name=rootvol --size=1000 --grow
```

2.10.3.1.11   System Details > File Preservation

If you have previously created a file preservation list, include this list as part of the Kickstart. This will protect the listed files from being over-written during the installation process. Refer to *Section 2.10.7, " Autoinstallation > File Preservation "* for information on how to create a file preservation list.

2.10.3.1.12   System Details > GPG & SSL

From this subtab, select the GPG keys and/or SSL certificates to be exported to the kickstarted system during the %post section of the Kickstart. For SUSE Manager customers, this list includes the SSL Certificate used during the installation of SUSE Manager.

 Note

> Any GPG key you wish to export to the kickstarted system must be in ASCII rather than binary format.

2.10.3.1.13   System Details > Troubleshooting

From this subtab, change information that may help with troubleshooting hardware problems:

Bootloader

> For some headless systems, it is better to select the non-graphic LILO bootloader.

Kernel Parameters

> Enter kernel parameters here that may help to narrow down the source of hardware issues.

2.10.3.1.14   Software > Package Groups

FIGURE 2.7: SOFTWARE

Figure 2.7, "Software" shows the subtabs that are available from the *Software* tab.

Enter the package groups, such as `@office` or `@admin-tools` you would like to install on the kickstarted system in the large text box. If you would like to know what package groups are available, and what packages they contain, refer to the `RedHat/base/` file of your Kickstart tree.

2.10.3.1.15 Software > Package Profiles

If you have previously created a Package Profile from one of your registered systems, you can use that profile as a template for the files to be installed on a kickstarted system. Refer to *Section 2.3.2.2, "System Details > Software > Packages"* for more information about package profiles.

2.10.3.1.16 Activation Keys

| Autoinstallation Details | System Details | Software | Activation Keys | Scripts | Autoinstallation File |

FIGURE 2.8: ACTIVATION KEYS

The *Activation Keys* tab allows you to select Activation Keys to include as part of the Kickstart profile. These keys, which must be created before the Kickstart profile, will be used when re-registering kickstarted systems.

2.10.3.1.17 Scripts

| Autoinstallation Details | System Details | Software | Activation Keys | Scripts | Autoinstallation File |

FIGURE 2.9: SCRIPTS

The *Scripts* tab is where %pre and %post scripts are created. This page lists any scripts that have already been created for this Kickstart profile. To create a new Kickstart script, perform the following procedure:

1. Click the *add new kickstart script* link in the upper right.

2. Enter the path to the scripting language used to create the script, such as `/usr/bin/perl`.

3. Enter the full script in the large text box.

4. Indicate whether this script is to be executed in the %pre or %post section of the Kickstart process.

5. Indicate whether this script is to run outside of the chroot environment. Refer to the *Post-installation Script* section of the *Red Hat Enterprise Linux System Administration Guide* for further explanation of the `nochroot` option.

 Note

SUSE Manager supports the inclusion of separate files within the Partition Details section of the Kickstart profile. For instance, you may dynamically generate a partition file based on the machine type and number of disks at Kickstart time. This file can be created via %pre script and placed on the system, such as `/tmp/part-include`. Then you can call for that file by entering the following line in the Partition Details field of the *System Details > Partitioning* tab:

```
%include /tmp/part-include
```

2.10.3.1.18 Autoinstallation File

Autoinstallation Details   System Details   Software   Activation Keys   Scripts   Autoinstallation File

FIGURE 2.10: AUTOINSTALLATION FILE

The *Autoinstallation File* tab allows you to view or download the profile that has been generated from the options chosen in the previous tabs.

2.10.3.2 Upload Kickstart/AutoYaST File

Click on the *Upload Kickstart/Autoyast File* link from the *Systems > Autoinstallation* page to upload an externally prepared AutoYaST or Kickstart profile.

1. In the first line, enter a profile *Label* for the automated installation. This label cannot contain spaces, so use dashes (-) or underscores (_) as separators.

2. Select an *Autoinstallable Tree* for this profile. The *Autoinstallable Tree* drop-down menu is only populated if one or more distributions have been created for the selected base channel (see *Section 2.10.6, "Autoinstallation > Distributions "*).

3. Instead of selecting a specific tree, you can also check the box *Always use the newest Tree for this base channel.* This setting lets SUSE Manager automatically pick the latest tree that is associated with the specified base channels. If you add new trees later, SUSE Manager will always keep the most recently created or modified.

4. Select the *Virtualization Type* from the drop-down menu.

 Note

> If you do not intend to use the autoinstall profile to create virtual guest systems, you can leave the drop-down set to the default choice *KVM Virtualized Guest.*

5. Finally, either provide the file contents with cut-and-paste or update the file from the local storage medium:

   - Paste it into the *File Contents* box and click *Create*, or

   - enter the file name in the *File to Upload* field and click *Upload File.*

Once done, four subtabs are available: *Details* (see *Section 2.10.3.1.8, " System Details > Details "*), *Bare Metal* (see *Section 2.10.3.1.7, " Autoinstallation Details > Bare Metal Autoinstallation "*),*Variables* (see *Section 2.10.3.1.3, " Autoinstallation Details > Variables "*), and *Autoinstallable File* (see *Section 2.10.3.1.18, "Autoinstallation File"*) are available.

2.10.4   Autoinstallation > Bare Metal

Lists the IP addresses that have been associated with the profiles created by your organization. Click either the range or the profile name to access different tabs of the *Autoinstallation Details* page.

2.10.5 Autoinstallation > GPG and SSL Keys

Lists keys and certificates available for inclusion in Kickstart profiles and provides a means to create new ones. This is especially important for customers of SUSE Manager or the Proxy Server because systems kickstarted by them must have the server key imported into SUSE Manager and associated with the relevant Kickstart profiles. Import it by creating a new key here and then make the profile association in the *GPG and SSL keys* subtab of the *Autoinstallation Details* page.

To create a new key or certificate, click the *Create Stored Key/Cert* link in the upper-right corner of the page. Enter a description, select the type, upload the file, and click the *Update Key* button. Note that a unique description is required.

 Important

> The GPG key you upload to SUSE Manager must be in ASCII format. Using a GPG key in binary format causes anaconda, and therefore the Kickstart process, to fail.

2.10.6 Autoinstallation > Distributions

The *Distributions* page enables you to find and create custom installation trees that may be used for automated installations.

 Note

> The *Distributions* page does not display distributions already provided. They can be found within the *Distribution* drop-down menu of the *Autoinstallation Details* page.
>
> Before creating a distribution, you must make an installation data available, as described in the *Automated Installation* chapter of the *SUSE Linux Enterprise Deployment Guide* (section *Simple Mass Installation*, "Providing the Installation Data") or, respectively, the *Kickstart Installations* chapter of the *Red Hat Enterprise Linux System Administration Guide*. This tree must be located in a local directory on the SUSE Manager server.

PROCEDURE 2.3: CREATING A DISTRIBUTION FOR AUTOINSTALLATION

1. To create a distribution, on the *Autoinstallable Distributions* page click *Create Distribution* in the upper right corner.

2. On the *Create Autoinstallable Distribution* page, provide the following data:

   a. Enter a label (without spaces) in the *Distribution Label* field, such as `my-orgs-sles-12-sp1` or `my-orgs-rhel-as-7`.

   b. In the *Tree Path* field, paste the path to the base of the installation tree. For Red Hat Enterprise Linux systems, you can test this by appending "images/pxeboot/README" to the URL in a Web browser, pressing `Enter`, and ensuring that the readme file appears.

   c. Select the matching distribution from the *Base Channel* and *Installer Generation* drop-down menus, such as `SUSE Linux` for SUSE Linux Enterprise, or `Red Hat Enterprise Linux 7` for Red Hat Enterprise Linux 7 client systems.

3. When finished, click the *Create Autoinstallable Distribution* button.

2.10.6.1 Autoinstallation > Distributions > Variables

Autoinstallation variables can be used to substitute values into Kickstart and AutoYaST profiles. To define a variable, create a name-value pair (*name/value*) in the text box.

For example, if you want to autoinstall a system that joins the network of a specified organization (for example the Engineering department) you can create a profile variable to set the IP address and the gateway server address to a variable that any system using that profile will use. Add the following line to the *Variables* text box.

```
IPADDR=192.168.0.28
GATEWAY=192.168.0.1
```

To use the distribution variable, use the name of the variable in the profile to substitute the value. For example, the `network` part of a Kickstart file looks like the following:

```
network --bootproto=static --device=eth0 --onboot=on --ip=$IPADDR \
  --gateway=$GATEWAY
```

The `$IPADDR` will be resolved to `192.168.0.28`, and the `$GATEWAY` to `192.168.0.1`.

Note

> There is a hierarchy when creating and using variables in Kickstart files. System Kickstart variables take precedence over Profile variables, which in turn take precedence over Distribution variables. Understanding this hierarchy can alleviate confusion when using variables in Kickstarts.

In AutoYaST profiles you can use such variables as well.

Using variables are just one part of the larger Cobbler infrastructure for creating templates that can be shared between multiple profiles and systems.

2.10.7 Autoinstallation > File Preservation

Collects lists of files to be protected and re-deployed on systems during Kickstart. For instance, if you have many custom configuration files located on a system to be kickstarted, enter them here as a list and associate that list with the Kickstart profile to be used.

To use this feature, click the *Create File Preservation List* link at the top. Enter a suitable label and all files and directories to be preserved. Enter absolute paths to all files and directories. Then click *Create List*.

 Important

> Although file preservation is useful, it does have limitations. Each list is limited to a total size of 1 MB. Special devices like `/dev/hda1` and `/dev/sda1` are not supported. Only file and directory names may be entered. No regular expression wildcards can be used.

When finished, you may include the file preservation list in the Kickstart profile to be used on systems containing those files. **Refer to** *Section 2.10.3.1, "Create a New Kickstart Profile"* **for precise** steps.

2.10.8 Autoinstallation > Autoinstallation Snippets

Use snippets to store common blocks of code that can be shared across multiple Kickstart or AutoYaST profiles in SUSE Manager.

2.10.8.1 Autoinstallation > Autoinstallation Snippets > Default Snippets

Default snippets coming with SUSE Manager are not editable. You can use a snippet, if you add the *Snippet Macro* statement such as `$SNIPPET('spacewalk/sles_register_script')` to your autoinstallation profile. This is an AutoYaST profile example:

```
<init-scripts config:type="list">
  $SNIPPET('spacewalk/sles_register_script')
</init-scripts>
```

When you create a snippet with the *Create Snippet* link, all profiles including that snippet will be updated accordingly.

2.10.8.2 Autoinstallation > Autoinstallation Snippets > Custom Snippets

This is the tab with custom snippets. Click a name of a snippet to view, edit, or delete it.

2.10.8.3 Autoinstallation > Autoinstallation Snippets > All Snippets

The *All Snippets* tab lists default and custom snippets together.

2.11 Software Crashes

2.12 Virtual Host Managers

3 Salt

If you click the *Salt* tab on the top navigation bar, by default the *Salt* › *Onboarding* view appears. On the left sidebar you can select *Remote Commands* to execute remote commands on your Salt Minions. You may also define a *States Catalog* for creating a collection of salt system states.

3.1 Onboarding

The *Onboarding* page provides a summary of your minions, including their names, fingerprints, current state, and actions you may perform on them.

Once you have pointed a minion to the SUSE Manager server as its master within */etc/salt/minion*, you can choose to accept or reject a minion from this page.

FIGURE 3.1: ONBOARDING OVERVIEW

3.2 Remote Commands

The remote commands page allows you to execute and run commands from the SUSE Manager server on minions.

 Warning: Remote Commands Security

All commands run from the `Remote Commands` page are executed as root on minions. As you may use wildcards to run commands across any number of systems you must always take extra precaution as this may have drastic consequences for your systems.

From the `Remote Commands` page within located under *Salt > Remote Commands* you will see two input fields. The first field is for entering commands. The second field is for targeting minions by name, group or by utilizing wildcards.

Enter the command you wish to execute, then enter the minion, group or wildcard you wish to execute the command on. Click the `Preview` button to check which machines will be targeted. Finally click the `Run` button to execute the command on the selected Salt managed systems.

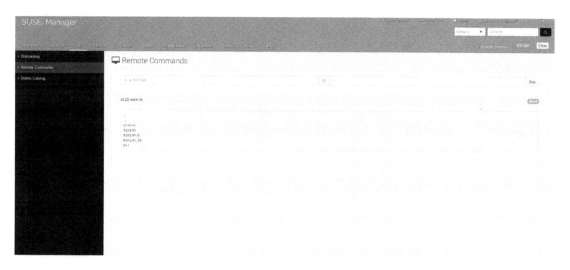

FIGURE 3.2: REMOTE COMMANDS

3.3 States Catalog

Selecting *Salt > States Catalog* brings you to the `States Catalog` overview. Use this page to manage your custom Salt states.

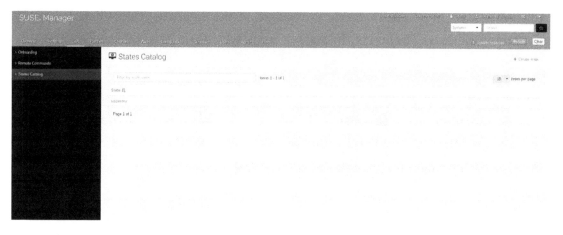

FIGURE 3.3: STATES CATALOG

Click the `+ Create State` button to open the `Create State` page. On this page you can define custom states which will be stored within the `State Catalog`. For example, to create a custom state for installation of the apache webserver you would provide a name: `Webserver` and the state content:

```
apache:
  pkg.installed: []
  service.running:
    - require:
      - pkg: apache
```

When you have finished entering your custom state definition click the `Create State` button. This will save the state and allow use of this specific state at the minion, group and organization level.

To add this state at the individual minion level perform the following actions:

PROCEDURE 3.1: USING A STATE WITH A MINION

1. From the *Systems* overview page, select a salt managed minion. You will be taken to the `System Details` page.

2. Select *States › Custom* from the navigation tabs.

3. Click the search button to look at an overview of all available states, or enter a custom state name to find it within the `States Catalog`.

4. Select the `Assign` checkbox to assign the state to this minion.

5. Click the `Save` button to save this assignment to the database. Then click the `Apply` button to finalize application of the state or states which you have selected.

 Note: The Save Button

The `Save` button saves your changes but does not apply the state. If you leave the page once clicking the save button your state will be saved to the database but not yet applied. You must apply states for all minions, groups or organizations for states to be finalized.

4 Patches

Select the *Patches* tab from the top navigation bar to track the availability and application of patches to your managed systems.

The *Patches Overview* page displays relevant patches for at least one of your managed systems that have not been applied yet.

 Note: Receiving Patches for Your System

> To receive an email when patches are issued for your system, go to *Overview ⟩ Your Preferences* and select *Receive email notifications*.

SUSE distinguishes three types of patches: security updates, bug fix updates, and enhancement updates. Each patch is comprised of a summary of the problem and solution, including the RPM packages fixing the problem.

Icons are used to identify the three types:

- 🛡 — Security Updates available, *strongly* recommended

- 🐛 — Bug Fix Updates available, recommended

- 🗗 — Enhancement Updates available, optional

A summary of each patch is provided in list form displaying the type, severity (for security updates), and subject of the patch, as well as the number of affected systems in your network.

In addition, you may view patches by product line at the following location: http://download.suse.com/patch/psdb/. For more information on security updates, see https://www.suse.com/support/security/.

4.1 Relevant Patches

The *Relevant* patches page displays a customized list of patches applying to your registered systems (see *Figure 4.1, "Relevant Patches"*). The list provides a summary of each patch, including its type, severity (for security updates), advisory number, synopsis, systems affected, and date updated.

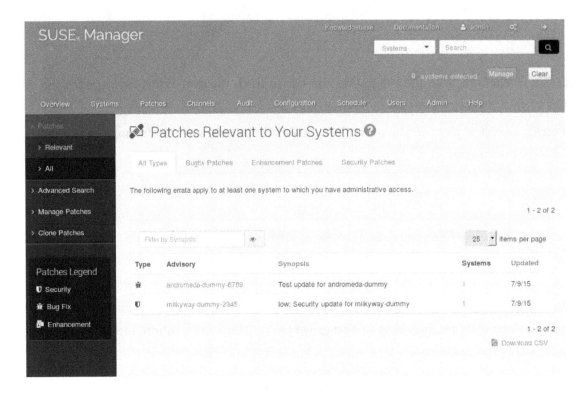

FIGURE 4.1: RELEVANT PATCHES

Clicking on a patch *Advisory* takes you to the *Details* page of the *Patch Details* page. Clicking on the number of associated systems takes you to the *Affected Systems* page of the *Patch Details* page. Refer to *Section 4.2.2, "Patch Details"* for more information.

4.2 All Patches

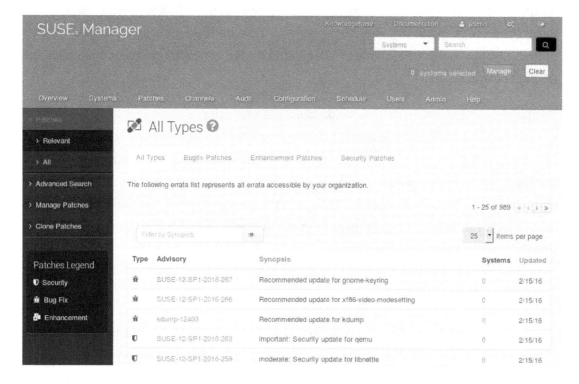

FIGURE 4.2: LIST OF ALL PATCHES

The *All Patches* page displays a list of all patches released by SUSE. Like in the *Relevant Patches* page, clicking either *Advisory* or the number of systems affected takes you to related tabs of the *Patch Details* page. Refer to *Section 4.2.2, "Patch Details"* for more information.

4.2.1 Apply Patches

Patches include a list of updated packages. To apply patches to a system, the system must be entitled.

Apply all applicable patches to a system by clicking on *Systems* › *Systems* in the top and left navigation bars. Click on the name of an entitled system. Then in the *System Details* page click the *Software* › *Patches* subtab. When the relevant patch list appears, click *Select All* then *Apply Patches* on the bottom right-hand corner of the page. Only patches not scheduled, scheduled but failed, or canceled patches are listed. Pending updates are excluded.

In addition, users with appropriate roles can apply patches using two other methods:

- To apply a specific patch to one or more systems, locate it in the patch list and click on the number of systems affected, which takes you to the *Affected Systems* page of the *Patch Details* page. Select the individual systems to be updated and click the *Apply Patches* button. Double-check the systems to be updated on the confirmation page, then click the *Confirm* button.

- To apply more than one patch to one or more systems, select the systems from the *Systems* list and click the *Update List* button. Click the *System Set Manager* link in the left navigation bar, then click the *Systems* tab. After ensuring the appropriate systems are selected, click the *Patch* tab, select the patches to apply, and click the *Apply Patch* button. Schedule a date and time for the patch to be applied. Default is the current date. Click the *Schedule Updates* button. You can follow the progress of the patch application via the *Pending Actions* list. Refer to *Chapter 8, Schedule* for more details.

! Important

If you use scheduled package installation, the packages or patches are installed via the SUSE Manager daemon. You must enable the SUSE Manager daemon on your systems.

The following rules apply to patches:

- Each package is a member of one or more channels. If a selected system is not subscribed to a channel containing the package, the update will not be installed on that system.

- If a newer version of the package is already installed on the system, the update will not be installed.

- If an older version of the package is installed, the package will be upgraded.

4.2.2   Patch Details

If you click on the advisory of a patch in the *Relevant* or *All* pages, its *Patch Details* page appears. This page is further divided into the following tabs:

4.2.2.1   *Patch Details > Details*

This subtab displays the patch report issued by SUSE. It provides a synopsis of the patch first, including the severity (for security updates), issue date, and any update dates. This is followed by a description of the patch and the steps required to resolve the issue.

Below the *Affected Channels* label, all channels that contain the affected package are listed. Clicking on a channel name displays the *Packages* subtab of the *Channel Details* page for that channel. Refer to *Section 5.1.9, "Software Channel Details"* for more information.

Security updates list the specific vulnerability as tracked by http://cve.mitre.org. This information is listed below the *CVEs* label.

OVAL is an open vulnerability and assessment language promoted by Mitre, http://oval.mitre.org. Clicking on the link below the *Oval* label downloads this information to your system. More useful are the collected SUSE Linux security updates on https://www.suse.com/support/update/.

4.2.2.2   *Patch Details > Packages*

This page provides links to each of the updated RPMs by channel. Clicking on the name of a package displays its *Package Details* page.

4.2.2.3   *Patch Details > Affected Systems*

This page lists systems affected by the patches. You can apply updates here. (See *Section 4.2.1, "Apply Patches"*.) Clicking on the name of a system takes you to its *System Details* page. Refer to *Section 2.3, "System Details"* for more information.

To determine whether an update has been scheduled, refer to the *Status* column in the affected systems table. Possible values are: N/A, Pending, Picked Up, Completed, and Failed. This column identifies only the last action related to a patch. For instance, if an action fails and you reschedule it, this column shows the status of the patch as pending with no mention of the previous failure. Clicking a status other than *N/A* takes you to the *Action Details* page. This column corresponds to one on the *Patch* tab of the *System Details* page.

4.3 Advanced Search

The *Patches Search* page allows you to search through patches by specific criteria.

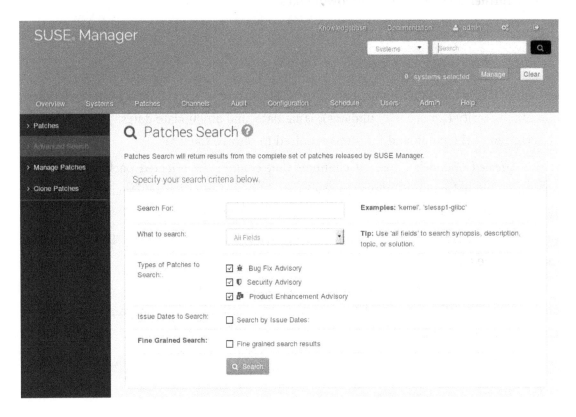

FIGURE 4.3: PATCHES SEARCH

- *All Fields* — Search patches by synopsis, description, topic, or solution.

- *Patch Advisory* — The name or the label of the patch.

- *Package Name* — Search particular packages by name:

```
kernel
```

Results will be grouped by advisory. For example, searching for 'kernel' returns all package names containing the string `kernel`, grouped by advisory.

- *CVE* — The name assigned to the security advisory by the Common Vulnerabilities and Exposures (CVE) project at http://cve.mitre.org. For example:

```
CVE-2006-4535
```

To filter patch search results, check or uncheck the boxes next to the type of advisory:

- Bug Fix Advisory — Patches that fix issues reported by users or discovered during development or testing.

- Security Advisory — Patches fixing a security issue found during development, testing, or reported by users or a software security clearing house. A security advisory usually has one or more CVE names associated with each vulnerability found in each package.

- Product Enhancement Advisory — Patches providing new features, improving functionality, or enhancing performance of a package.

4.4 Manage Patches

Custom patches enable organizations to issue patch alerts for the packages in their custom channels, schedule deployment and manage patches across organizations.

 Warning

> If the organization is using both SUSE Manager and SUSE Manager Proxy, manage patches only on the SUSE Manager since the proxy servers receive updates directly from it. Managing patches on a proxy in this combined configuration risks putting your servers out of sync.

Patch management distinguishes between published and unpublished patches.

- *Published*: displays the patch alerts the organization has created and disseminated. To edit an existing published patch, follow the steps described in *Section 4.4.1, "Creating and Editing Patches"*. To distribute the patch, click *Send Notification* on the top-right corner of the *Patch Details* page. The patch alert is sent to the administrators of all affected systems.

- *Unublished*: displays the patch alerts your organization has created but not yet distributed. To edit an existing unpublished patch, follow the steps described in *Section 4.4.1, "Creating and Editing Patches"*. To publish the patch, click *Publish Patch* on the top-right corner of the *Patch Details* page. Confirm the channels associated with the patch and click the *Publish Patch* button, now in the lower-right corner. The patch alert is moved to the *Published* page awaiting distribution.

4.4.1 Creating and Editing Patches

To create a custom patch alert, proceed as follows:

1. On the top navigation bar, click on *Patches*, then select *Manage Patches* on the left navigation bar. On the *Patch Management* page, click *Create Patch*.

2. Enter a label for the patch in the *Advisory* field, ideally following a naming convention adopted by your organization.

3. Complete all remaining required fields, then click the *Create Patch* button. View standard SUSE Alerts for examples of properly completed fields.

SUSE Manager administrators can also create patches by cloning an existing one. Cloning preserves package associations and simplifies issuing patches. See *Section 4.5, "Cloning Patches"* for instructions.

To edit an existing patch alert's details, click its advisory on the *Patch Management* page, make the changes in the appropriate fields of the *Details* tab, and click the *Update Patch* button. Click on the *Channels* tab to alter the patch's channel association. Click on the *Packages* tab to view and modify its packages.

To delete patches, select their check boxes on the *Patch Management* page, click the *Delete Patch* button, and confirm the action. Deleting published patches might take a few minutes.

4.4.2 Assigning Packages to Patches

To assign packages to patches, proceed as follows:

1. Select a patch, click on the *Packages* tab, then the *Add* subtab.

2. To associate packages with the patch being edited, select the channel from the *View* drop-down menu that contains the packages and click *View*. Packages already associated with the patch being edited are not displayed. Selecting *All managed packages* presents all available packages.

3. After clicking *View*, the package list for the selected option appears. Note that the page header still lists the patch being edited.

4. In the list, select the check boxes of the packages to be assigned to the edited patch and click *Add Packages* at the bottom-right corner of the page.

5. A confirmation page appears with the packages listed. Click *Confirm* to associate the packages with the patch. The *List/Remove* subtab of the *Managed Patch Details* page appears with the new packages listed.

Once packages are assigned to a patch, the patch cache is updated to reflect the changes. This update is delayed briefly so that users may finish editing a patch before all the changes are made available. To initiate the changes to the cache manually, follow the directions to *commit the changes immediately* at the top of the page.

4.4.3   Publishing Patches

After adding packages to the patch, the patch needs to be published to be disseminated to affected systems. Follow this procedure to publish patches:

1. On the top navigation bar, click on *Patches*, then *Manage Patches* on the left navigation bar.

2. Click on *Publish Patch*. A confirmation page appears that will ask you to select which channels you wish to make the patch available in. Choose the relevant channels.

3. Click *Publish Patch*. The patch published will now appear on the *Published* page of *Manage Patches*.

4.5   Cloning Patches

Patches can be cloned for easy replication and distribution as part of SUSE Manager. Only patches potentially applicable to one of your channels can be cloned. Patches can be applicable to a channel if that channel was cloned from a channel to which the patch applies. To access this functionality, click *Patches* on the top navigation bar, then *Clone Patches* on the left navigation bar.

On the *Clone Patches* page, select the channel containing the patch from the *View* drop-down menu and click *View*. Once the patch list appears, select the check box of the patch to be cloned and click *Clone Patch*. A confirmation page appears with the patch listed. Click *Confirm* to finish cloning.

The cloned patch appears in the *Unpublished* patch list. Verify the patch text and the packages associated with that patch, then publish the patch so it is available to users in your organization.

5 Channels

If you click the *Channels* tab on the top navigation bar, the *Channels* category and links appear. The pages in the *Channels* category enable you to view and manage the channels and packages associated with your systems.

For more information about channel management, see *Book "SUSE Manager Best Practices", Chapter 4 "Channel Management", Section 4.1 "Introduction"*.

5.1 Software Channels

The *Software Channels* page is the first to appear in the *Channels* category. A software channel provides packages grouped by products or applications to ease the selection of packages to be installed on a system.

There are two types of software channels: base channels and child channels.

5.1.1 Base Channels

A base channel consists of packages built for a specific architecture and release. For example, all of the packages in SUSE Linux Enterprise Server 12 for the x86_64 architecture make up a base channel. The list of packages in SUSE Linux Enterprise Server 12 for the s390x architecture make up a different base channel.

A system must be subscribed to only one base channel assigned automatically during registration based on the SUSE Linux Enterprise release and system architecture. In case of paid base channels, an associated subscription must exist.

5.1.2 Child Channels

A child channel is associated with a base channel and provides extra packages. For instance, an organization can create a child channel associated with SUSE Linux Enterprise Server on x86_64 architecture that contains extra packages for a custom application.

A system can be subscribed to multiple child channels of its base channel. Only packages provided by a subscribed channel can be installed or updated. SUSE Manager Administrators and Channel Administrators have channel management authority. This authority gives them the ability to create and manage their own custom channels.

 Note

Do not create child channels containing packages that are not compatible with the client system.

Channels can be further distinguished by relevance: *All Channels*, *SUSE Channels*, *Popular Channels*, *My Channels*, *Shared Channels*, and *Retired Channels*.

5.1.3 All Channels

Under *Software Channels* in the left navigation bar click *All Channels* to reach the page shown in *Figure 5.1, "All Channels"*. All channels available to your organization are listed. Links within this list go to different tabs of the *Software Channel Details* page. Clicking on a channel name takes you to the *Details* tab. Clicking on the number of packages takes you to the *Packages* tab. Clicking on the number of systems takes you to the *Subscribed Systems* tab. Refer to *Section 5.1.9, "Software Channel Details"* for details.

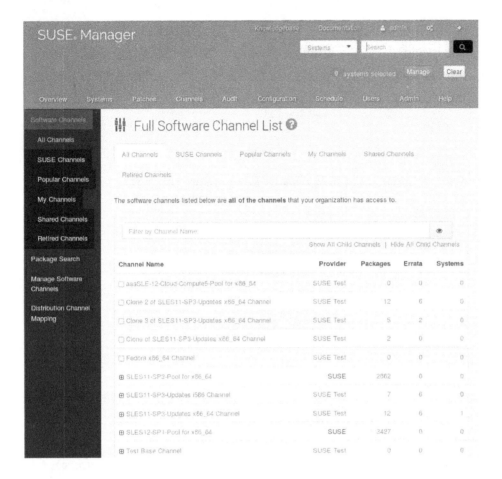

FIGURE 5.1: ALL CHANNELS

5.1.4   SUSE Channels

The *SUSE Channels* page displays the SUSE channels and their available child channels.

 Warning: SUSE Channels Cannot be Deleted

Once imported, SUSE channels cannot be deleted. Only custom software channels can be deleted.

5.1.5 Popular Channels

The *Popular Channels* page displays the software channels most subscribed by systems registered to your organization. You can refine the search by using the drop-down menu to list only the channels with at least a certain number of systems subscribed.

5.1.6 My Channels

The *My Channels* page displays all software channels that belong to your organization, including both SUSE and custom channels. Use the text box to filter by channel name.

5.1.7 Shared Channels

The *Shared Channels* page displays the channels shared with others in the organizational trust.

5.1.8 Retired Channels

The *Retired Channels* page displays available channels that have reached their end-of-life dates and do not receive updates.

5.1.9 Software Channel Details

If you click on the name of a channel, the *Software Channel Details* page appears. Here the following tabs are available:

5.1.9.1 Software Channel Details > Details

General information about the channel and its parent if applicable. This summary, description, and architecture is also displayed when clicking on a channel.

In addition, *Per-User Subscription Restrictions* can be set globally by SUSE Manager administrators and channel administrators. By default, any user can subscribe channels to a system. To manage user permissions, select *Only selected users within your organization may subscribe to this channel* and click *Update*. The *Subscribers* tab appears. Click on it to grant specific users subscription permissions to a channel. SUSE Manager administrators and channel administrators can always subscribe any channels to a system.

Only customers with custom base channels can change their systems' base channel assignments via the SUSE Manager Web interface in two ways:

- Assign the system to a custom base channel.

- Revert subscriptions from a custom base channel to the appropriate distribution-based base channel.

 Note

> The assigned base channel must match the installed system. For example, a system running SUSE Linux Enterprise 11 for x86_64 cannot be registered to a SUSE Linux Enterprise 12 for s390x base channel. Use the files `/etc/os-release` or `/etc/SuSE-release` to check your product, architecture (try **uname -a**), version, and patch level.

5.1.9.2   Software Channel Details > Managers

On the *Managers* page, you can check which users are authorized to manage the selected channel. Real name and email address are listed with the user names. Organization and Channel administrators can manage any channel. As a SUSE Manager administrator you can change roles for specific users by clicking on the name. For more information on user management and the *User Details* page, see *Chapter 9, Users*.

5.1.9.3   Software Channel Details > Patches

This page lists patches to be applied to packages provided in the channel. The list displays advisory types, names, summaries, and issue dates. Clicking on an advisory name takes you to its *Patch Details* page. Refer to *Section 4.2.2, "Patch Details"* for more information.

5.1.9.4 *Software Channel Details > Packages*

This page lists packages in the channel. Clicking on a package name takes you to the *Package Details* page. This page displays a set of tabs with information about the package, including architectures on which it runs, the package size, build date, package dependencies, change log, list of files in the package, newer versions, and which systems have the package installed. Download the packages as RPMs.

To search for a specific package or a subset of packages, use the package filter at the top of the list. Enter a substring to search for package names containing the string. For example, typing `dd` in the filter might return: `dd_rescue`, `ddclient`, and `uuidd`. The filter is case-insensitive.

5.1.9.5 *Software Channel Details > Subscribed Systems*

The list displays system names, base channels, and their system type. Clicking on a system name takes you to its *System Details* page. Refer to *Section 2.3, "System Details"* for more information.

In case of a child channel, you have the option to unsubscribe systems from this channel. Use the check boxes to select the systems, then click the *Unsubscribe* button.

5.1.9.6 *Software Channel Details > Target Systems*

List of systems eligible for subscription to the channel. This tab appears only for child channels. Use the check boxes to select the systems, then click the *Confirm* and *Subscribe* button on the bottom right-hand corner. You will receive a success message or be notified of any errors. This can also be accomplished through the *Channels* tab of the *System Details* page. Refer to *Section 2.3, "System Details"* for more information.

5.2 Package Search

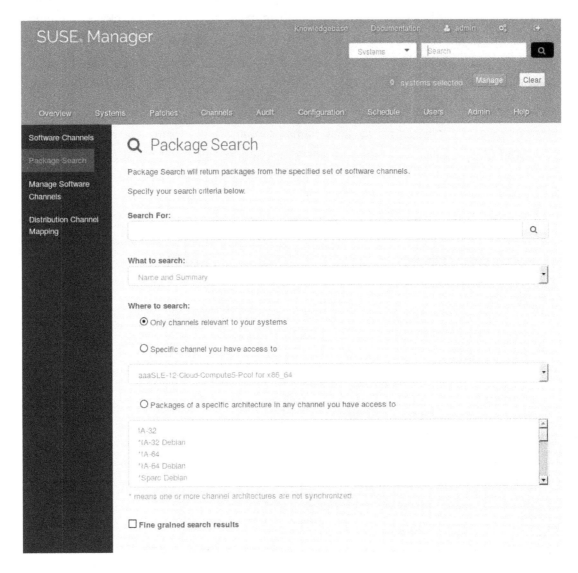

FIGURE 5.2: PACKAGE SEARCH

The *Package Search* page allows you to search through packages using various criteria (provided by the *What to search for* selection list):

- *Free Form* — a general keyword search useful when the details of a particular package and its contents are unknown.

- *Name Only* — Targeted search to find a specific package known by name.

- *Name and Summary* — Search for a package or program which might not show up in the respective package name but in its one-line summary.

- *Name and Description* — Search package names and their descriptions. Search results for "web browser" include both graphical and text-based browsers.

The *Free Form* field additionally allows you to search using field names that you prepend to search queries and filter results by that field keyword.

For example, if you wanted to search all of the SUSE Linux Enterprise packages for the word `java` in the description and summary, type the following in the *Free Form* field:

```
summary:java and description:java
```

Other supported field names include:

- `name`: search package names for a particular keyword,

- `version`: search for a particular package version,

- `filename`: search the package filenames for a particular keyword,

- `description`: search the packages' detailed descriptions for a particular keyword,

- `summary`: search the packages' brief summary for a particular keyword,

- `arch`: search the packages by their architecture (such as x86_64, ppc64le, or s390).

You can also limit searches to *Channels relevant to your systems* by clicking the check box. Additionally, you can restrict your search by platform (*Specific channel you have access to*) or architecture (*Packages of a specific architecture ...*).

5.3 Manage Software Channels

This tab allows administrators to create, clone, and delete custom channels. These channels may contain altered versions of distribution-based channels or custom packages.

5.3.1 *Manage Software Channels > Channel Details*

The default screen of the *Manage Software Channels* tab lists all available channels including custom, distribution-based, and child channels.

To clone an existing channel, click the *Clone Channel* link. Select the channel to be cloned from the drop-down menu, select whether to clone the current state (including patches) or the original state (without patches). You can also select specific patches to use for cloning. Then click the *Create Channel* button. In the next screen select options for the new channel, including base architecture and GPG, then click *Create Channel*.

To create a new channel, click the *Create Channel* link. Select the appropriate options for the new channel, including base architecture and GPG options, then click *Create Channel*. Note that a channel created in this manner is blank, containing no packages. You must either upload software packages or add packages from other repositories. You may also choose to include patches in your custom channel.

5.3.1.1 Manage Software Channels > Channel Details > Details

This screen lists the selections made during channel creation.

5.3.1.2 Manage Software Channels > Channel Details > Managers

SUSE Manager administrators and channel administrators may alter or delete any channel. To grant other users rights to alter or delete this channel, check the box next to the user's name and click *Update*.

To allow all users to manage the channel, click the *Select All* button at the bottom of the list then click *Update*. To remove a user's right to manage the channel, uncheck the box next to their name and click *Update*.

5.3.1.3 Manage Software Channels > Channel Details > Patches

Channel managers can list, remove, clone, and add patches to their custom channel. Custom channels not cloned from a distribution may not contain patches until packages are available. Only patches that match the base architecture and apply to a package in that channel may be added. Finally, only cloned or custom patches may be added to custom channels. Patches may be included in a cloned channel if they are selected during channel creation.

The *Sync* tab lists patches that were updated since they were originally cloned in the selected cloned channel. More specifically, a patch is listed here if and only if:

- it is a cloned patch,

- it belongs to the selected cloned channel,

- it has already been published in the selected cloned channel,

- it does not contain a package that the original patch has, or it has at least one package with a different version with respect to the corresponding one in the original patch, or both.

Clicking on the *Sync Patches* button opens a confirmation page in which a subset of those patches can be selected for synchronization. Clicking on the *Confirm* button in the confirmation page results in such patches being copied over from the original channel to the cloned channel, thus updating corresponding packages.

5.3.1.4   *Manage Software Channels > Channel Details > Packages*

As with patches, administrators can list, remove, compare, and add packages to a custom channel.

To list all packages in the channel, click the *List / Remove Packages* link. Check the box to the left of any package you wish to remove, then click *Remove Packages*.

To add packages, click the *Add Packages* link. From the drop down menu choose a channel from which to add packages and click *View* to continue. Check the box to the left of any package you wish to add to the custom channel, then click *Add Packages*.

To compare packages in the current channel with those in another, select that channel from the drop-down menu and click *Compare*. Packages in both channels are compared, including architecture and version. The results are displayed on the next screen.

To make the two channels identical, click the *Merge Differences* button. In the next dialog, resolve any conflicts. *Preview Merge* allows you to review the changes before applying them to the channels. Select those packages that you wish to merge. Click *Merge Packages* then *Confirm* to perform the merge.

5.3.1.5 *Manage Software Channels > Channel Details > Repositories*

On the *Repositories* page, assign software repositories to the channel and synchronize repository content:

- *Add/Remove* lists configured repositories, which can be added and removed by selecting the check box next to the repository name and clicking *Update Repositories*.

- *Sync* lists configured repositories. The synchronization schedule can be set using the drop-down boxes, or an immediate synchronization can be performed by clicking *Sync Now*.

The *Manage Repositories* tab to the left shows all assigned repositories. Click on a name to see details and possibly delete a repository.

5.3.2 *Manage Software Channels > Manage Software Packages*

To manage custom software packages, list all software or view only packages in a custom channel. Select the respective channel from the drop-down menu and click *View Packages*.

5.3.3 *Manage Software Channels > Manage Repositories*

Add or manage custom or third-party package repositories and link the repositories to an existing channel. The repositories feature currently supports repomd repositories.

To create a new repository click the *Create Repository* link at the top right of the *Manage Repositories* page. The *Create Repository* screen prompts you to enter a *Repository Label* such as `sles-12-x86_64` and a *Repository URL*. You may enter URLs pointing to mirror lists or direct download repositories, then click *Create Repository*.

To link the new repository to an existing software channel, select *Manage Software Channels* from the left menu, then click the channel you want to link. In the channel's detail page, click the *Repositories* subtab, then check the box next to the repository you want to link to the channel. Click *Update Repositories*.

To synchronize packages from a custom repository to your channel, click the *Sync* link from the channel's *Repositories* subtab, and confirm by clicking the *Sync* button.

You can also perform a sync via command-line by using the `spacewalk-repo-sync` command, which additionally allows you to accept keys.

`spacewalk-repo-sync` creates log files in the `/var/log/rhn/reposync` directory. SUSE Manager uses one log file per channel and reuses it with the next sync run.

5.4 Distribution Channel Mapping

6 Audit

Select the *Audit* tab from the top navigation bar to audit your managed systems.

6.1 CVE Audit

The *CVE Audit* page will display a list of client systems with their patch status regarding a given CVE (Common Vulnerabilities and Exposures) number.

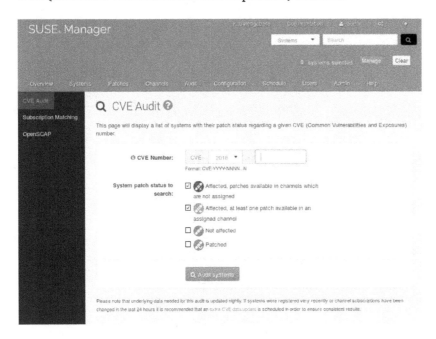

FIGURE 6.1: CVE AUDIT

6.1.1 Normal Usage

Proceed as follows if you want to verify that a client system has received a given CVE patch:

1. Make sure that the CVE data is up-to-date. For more information, see *Section 6.1.3, "Maintaining CVE Data"*.

2. Click the *Audit* tab to open the *CVE Audit* page.

3. Input a 13-char CVE identifier in the *CVE Number* field. The year setting will be automatically adjusted. Alternatively, set the year manually and add the last four digits.

4. Optionally, uncheck the patch statuses you are not interested in.

5. Click *Audit systems*.

Then a list of client systems is displayed, where each system comes with a *Patch Status* describing its situation regarding the given CVE identifier. Possible statuses are:

[red] Affected, patches are available in channels that are not assigned:
> The system is affected by the vulnerability and SUSE Manager has one or more patches for it, but at this moment, the channels offering the patches are not assigned to the system.

[orange] Affected, at least one patch available in an assigned channel:
> The system is affected by the vulnerability, SUSE Manager has at least one patch for it in a channel that is directly assigned to the system.

[grey] Not affected:
> The system does not have any packages installed that are patchable.

[green] Patched:
> A patch has already been installed.

- More than one patch might be needed to fix a certain vulnerability.

- The [orange] state is displayed as soon as SUSE Manager has at least one patch in an assigned channel. This might mean that, after installing such patch, others might be needed —users should double check the CVE Audit page after applying a patch to be sure that their systems are not affected anymore.

For a more precise definitions of these states, see *Section 6.1.4, "Tips and Background Information"*.

 Note: Unknown CVE Number
> If the CVE number is not known to SUSE Manager, an error message is displayed because SUSE Manager is unable to collect and display any audit data.

For each system, the *Next Action* column contains suggestions on the steps to take in order to address the vulnerabilities. Under these circumstances it is either sensible to install a certain patch or assign a new channel. If applicable, a list of "candidate" channels or patches is displayed for your convenience.

You can also assign systems to a *System Set* for further batch processing.

6.1.2 API Usage

An API method called `audit.listSystemsByPatchStatus` is available to run CVE audits from custom scripts. Details on how to use it are available in the API guide.

6.1.3 Maintaining CVE Data

To produce correct results, CVE Audit must periodically refresh the data needed for the search in the background. By default, the refresh is scheduled at 11:00 PM every night. It is recommended to run such a refresh right after the SUSE Manager installation to get proper results immediately instead of waiting until the next day.

1. In the Web interface, click the *Admin* tab.

2. Click *Task Schedules* in the left menu.

3. Click the `cve-server-channels-default` schedule link.

4. Click the `cve-server-channels-bunch` link.

5. Click the *Single Run Schedule* button.

6. After some minutes, refresh the page and check that the scheduled run status is `FINISHED`.

A direct link is also available in the *CVE Audit* tab.

6.1.4 Tips and Background Information

Audit results are only correct if the assignment of channels to systems did not change since the last scheduled refresh (normally at 11:00 PM every night). If a CVE audit is needed and channels were assigned or unassigned to any system during the day, a manual run is recommended. For more information, see *Section 6.1.3, "Maintaining CVE Data"*.

Systems are called "affected", "not affected" or "patched" not in an absolute sense, but based on information available to SUSE Manager. This implies that concepts such as "being affected by a vulnerability" have particular meanings in this context. The following definitions apply:

System affected by a certain vulnerability:

A system which has an installed package with version lower than the version of the same package in a relevant patch marked for the vulnerability.

System not affected by a certain vulnerability:
> A system which has no installed package that is also in a relevant patch marked for the vulnerability.

System patched for a certain vulnerability:
> A system which has an installed package with version equal to or greater than the version of the same package in a relevant patch marked for the vulnerability.

Relevant patch:
> A patch known by SUSE Manager in a relevant channel.

Relevant channel:
> A channel managed by SUSE Manager, which is either assigned to the system, the original of a cloned channel which is assigned to the system, a channel linked to a product which is installed on the system or a past or future service pack channel for the system.

A notable consequence of the above definitions is that results can be incorrect in cases of unmanaged channels, unmanaged packages, or non-compliant systems.

6.2 Subscription Matching in SUSE Manager 3

To match subscriptions with your systems utilize the new subscription-matcher tool. It gathers information about systems, subscriptions and pinned matches (fixed customer defined subscriptions to systems mapping) as input and returns the best possible match according to the SUSE Terms and Conditions. The subscription-matcher is also able to write some CSV Reports:

* The `Subscriptions Report` provides subscriptions report data when used

* The `Unmatched Products Report` provides information on products and their systems when a match to a subscription cannot be found

* The `Error Report` provides a list of errors raised during the matching process

Selecting *Audit > Subscription Matching* from the left navigation bar will provide you with an overview of all results generated by the Subscription Matcher. The Subscription Matcher helps provide visual coverage on subscription usage and enable more accurate reporting.

! Important: Subscription Matcher Accuracy

This tool's goal is to help provide visual coverage on current subscription use and enable more accurate reporting. The `Subscription Matcher` is excellent at matching systems and products registered with SUSE Manager however any systems, products or environments which are not found in the database will remain unmatched. This tool was never intended to act as a replacement for auditing. Auditing should always take precedence over subscription matching.

Note: Coexistence of virtual-host-gather and Poller

virtual-host-gatherer should not be used for gathering the data from hypervisors that are registered systems in SUSE Manager (running SLES or RES). Information from these hypervisors has already been retrieved using the poller utility and redundant information from virtual-host-gatherer may cause conflicts.

The Subscription Matching overview provides subscription part numbers, product descriptions, policies, matched total subscriptions used and remaining, and the start and end dates of subscriptions.

FIGURE 6.2: SUBSCRIPTION MATCHING OVERVIEW

Matched/Total

If the total amounts of a subscription are fully matched, the quantity column value is

highlighted with a yellow warning triangle:

Expiration Warning

When a subscription will expire within less than 3 months, the record is highlighted

Expired Subscriptions

If a subscription is expired, the record for it is faded

6.2.1 Subscription Matcher Reports

SUSE Manager 3 automatically generates up-to-date nightly status reports by matching your SUSE subscriptions with all your registered systems. These reports are stored in `/var/lib/spacewalk/subscription-matcher` and provided in CSV format. These CSV files may be opened with any mainstream spreadsheet application such as LibreOffice Calc.

If you would like to schedule these reports to be produced at different times, or a at a certain frequency or schedule a one time completion you can perform this task by editing the Taskomatic settings for the gatherer-matcher located under Schedule name at: *Admin > Task Schedules > gatherer-matcher-default*

FIGURE 6.3: GATHERER-MATCHER-DEFAULT

6.2.2 Unmatched Systems

Selecting the *Subscription Matching* › *Unmatched Products* tab provides an overview of all systems the matcher could not find in the database or which were not registered with SUSE Manager. The `Unmatched Products` overview contains product names and the number of unmatched systems which remain unmatched with known installed products.

FIGURE 6.4: UNMATCHED PRODUCTS

Show System List

Select to open and display a list of all systems which were detected with an installed product but remain unmatched with a subscription.

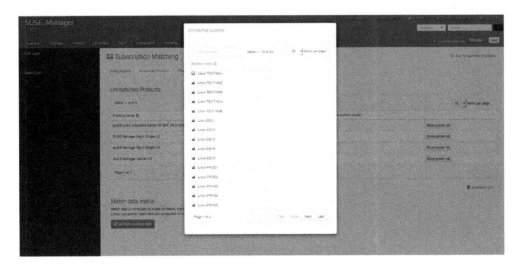

FIGURE 6.5: SHOW SYSTEM LIST

6.2.3   Subscription Pinning

The Subscription Pinning feature allows a user to instruct the subscription-matcher to favour matching a specific subscription with a given system or group of systems. This is achieved by creating Pins. Each pin contains information about the preferred subscription-system match.

 Note: Respecting Pins

> In some cases the algorithm may determine that a specific pin cannot be respected, depending on the subscription's availability and applicability rules, in this case it will be shown as not satisfied.

The Pins table displays a list of all pins. Items in the list contain the status of pins, which can be `satisfied`, `not satisfied` and `pending next run`.

- A pin is `Satisfied` if its system and subscription was matched in the last matcher run

- A pin is `Not Satisfied` if its system and subscription was *NOT* matched in the last matcher run. This can happen, for example, if the pin violates terms and conditions for subscriptions.

- A Pin is in the `Pending Next Run` state when it needs a new matcher run to be taken into account. After the new run, the pin will become either `Satisfied` or `Not Satisfied`.

FIGURE 6.6: SUBSCRIPTION PINNING

Click the + Add a Pin button to open the *Available Systems* window. You may filter systems by name and select a system for the matcher to pin manually.

Add a Pin

Step 1/2: select the system to pin from the table below.

Filter by name		Items 1 - 5 of 232	5 ▾ items per page
System ⬍	**Socket/IFL count**	**Products**	
🖥 Linux-QA1	1	SUSE Manager Mgmt Single 1.2. ...	Select →
📦 Linux-QA2	1	SUSE Manager Mgmt Single 1.2, ...	Select →
📦 Linux-QA3	1		Select →
📦 Linux-QA4	2	SUSE Manager Mgmt Single 1.2. ...	Select →
📦 Linux-Marketing1	2	SUSE Manager Mgmt Single 1.2. ...	Select →
Page 1 of 47			First Prev Next Last

FIGURE 6.7: ADD A PIN

Within the *Subscriptions Available for Selected System* window click the Save Pin button to raise priority for subscription use on the selected system.

6.2.4 Subscription Matching Messages

You can review all messages related to Subscription Matching from the *Subscription Matching › Messages* overview.

FIGURE 6.8: ADD A PIN

6.2.5   Virtual Host Managers

A pre-requirement for matching subscriptions with systems is to have complete information covering which virtual systems are running on which virtual host. SUSE Manager gets this information without any further configuration if the hypervisor is a registered system running on SUSE Linux Enterprise Server or RedHat Enterprise Linux. Third party hypervisors, like VMware or Hyper-V, will need further configuration as described in this chapter.

Third party hypervisors and hypervisor managers such as VMWare vCenter are called "Virtual Host Managers" (VHM) within SUSE Manager, as they are able to manage one or multiple virtual hosts, which in turn may contain virtual guests. SUSE Manager 3 ships with a tool `virtual-host-gatherer` that can connect to VHMs using their API, and request information about virtual hosts. This tool is automatically invoked via Taskomatic nightly, therefore you need to configure your VHMs via XMLRPC APIs. `virtual-host-gatherer` maintains the concept of optional modules, where each module enables a specific Virtual Host Manager.

On the *Subscription Matching* overview select *Edit Virtual Host Managers*. This will take you to the *Systems › Virtual Host Managers* overview. In the upper right you can select either + *Add VMware-based Virtual Host Manager* or + *Add File-based Virtual Host Manager*. These modules allow you to match subscriptions to machines managed by a virtual host such as `VMware`, `ESX`, `ESXi` and `vCenter`. If using an unsupported virtual host you can also create a custom json file to provide `virtual-host-gatherer` with the required host/guest information.

6.2.5.1 VMware-based Virtual Host Manager

Select `VMware-based Virtual Host Manager` to enter the location of your VMware-based virtual host. Enter a `Label:`, `Hostname:`, `Port:`, `Username:` and `Password:`. Finally click the `+ Add Virtual Host Manager` button.

FIGURE 6.9: VMWARE-BASED VIRTUAL HOST MANAGER

6.2.5.2 File Based Virtual Host Manager

If you are using an unsupported virtual host manager, you can create and use a file formatted in json containing information about a host and all managed guest machines. Select `+ File Based Virtual Host Manager` then enter a label and URL leading to the location of this file for the virtual-host-gatherer

The following json example describes how this file should look:

```
$> virtual-host-gatherer --infile infile.json
    {
            "examplevhost": {
                "10.11.12.13": {
                    "cpuArch": "x86_64",
                    "cpuDescription": "AMD Opteron(tm) Processor 4386",
                    "cpuMhz": 3092.212727,
                    "cpuVendor": "amd",
                    "hostIdentifier": "'vim.HostSystem:host-182'",
                    "name": "11.11.12.13",
                    "os": "VMware ESXi",
                    "osVersion": "5.5.0",
```

```
        "ramMb": 65512,
        "totalCpuCores": 16,
        "totalCpuSockets": 2,
        "totalCpuThreads": 16,
        "type": "vmware",
        "vms": {
            "vCenter": "564d6d90-459c-2256-8f39-3cb2bd24b7b0"
        }
    },
    "10.11.12.14": {
        "cpuArch": "x86_64",
        "cpuDescription": "AMD Opteron(tm) Processor 4386",
        "cpuMhz": 3092.212639,
        "cpuVendor": "amd",
        "hostIdentifier": "'vim.HostSystem:host-183'",
        "name": "10.11.12.14",
        "os": "VMware ESXi",
        "osVersion": "5.5.0",
        "ramMb": 65512,
        "totalCpuCores": 16,
        "totalCpuSockets": 2,
        "totalCpuThreads": 16,
        "type": "vmware",
        "vms": {
            "49737e0a-c9e6-4ceb-aef8-6a9452f67cb5":
"4230c60f-3f98-2a65-f7c3-600b26b79c22",
            "5a2e4e63-a957-426b-bfa8-4169302e4fdb":
"42307b15-1618-0595-01f2-427ffcddd88e",
            "NSX-gateway": "4230d43e-aafe-38ba-5a9e-3cb67c03a16a",
            "NSX-l3gateway": "4230b00f-0b21-0e9d-dfde-6c7b06909d5f",
            "NSX-service": "4230e924-b714-198b-348b-25de01482fd9"
        }
    }
  }
}
```

For more information see the man page on your SUSE Manager server for virtual-host-gatherer:

```
# man virtual-host-gatherer
```

6.2.6 Configuring Virtual Host Managers via XMLRPC API

The following APIs allow you to get a list of available virtual-host-manager modules and the parameters they require:

- virtualhostmanager.listAvailableVirtualHostGathererModules(session)

- virtualhostmanager.getModuleParameters(session, moduleName)

The following APIs allow you to create and delete VHMs. Take care that the module parameter map must match the map returned by virtualhostmanager.getModuleParameters to work correctly:

- virtualhostmanager.create(session, label, moduleName, parameters)

- virtualhostmanager.delete(session, label)

The following APIs return information about configured VHMs:

- virtualhostmanager.listVirtualHostManagers(session)

- virtualhostmanager.getDetail(session, label)

6.3 OpenSCAP

If you click the *OpenSCAP* tab on the left navigation bar, an overview of the OpenSCAP Scans appears. SCAP (Security Content Automation Protocol) is a framework to maintain the security of enterprise systems. It mainly performs the following tasks:

- automatically verifies the presence of patches,

- checks system security configuration settings,

- examines systems for signs of compromise.

For a description of the Web interface dialogs, see *Section 6.4.5, "OpenSCAP SUSE Manager Web Interface"*.

For instructions and tips on how to best use OpenSCAP with SUSE Manager, refer to *Section 6.4, "System Security via OpenSCAP"*. To learn more about OpenSCAP check out the project homepage at http://open-scap.org.

6.4 System Security via OpenSCAP

The Security Certification and Authorization Package (SCAP) is a standardized compliance checking solution for enterprise-level Linux infrastructures. It is a line of specifications maintained by the National Institute of Standards and Technology (NIST) for maintaining system security for enterprise systems.

SUSE Manager uses OpenSCAP to implement the SCAP specifications. OpenSCAP is an auditing tool that utilizes the Extensible Configuration Checklist Description Format (XCCDF). XCCDF is a standard way of expressing checklist content and defines security checklists. It also combines with other specifications such as Common Platform Enumeration (CPE), Common Configuration Enumeration (CCE), and Open Vulnerability and Assessment Language (OVAL), to create a SCAP-expressed checklist that can be processed by SCAP-validated products.

6.4.1 OpenSCAP Features

OpenSCAP verifies the presence of patches by using content produced by the SUSE Security Team (https://www.suse.com/support/security/), checks system security configuration settings and examines systems for signs of compromise by using rules based on standards and specifications.

To effectively use OpenSCAP, the following must be available:

A tool to verify a system confirms to a standard

SUSE Manager uses OpenSCAP as an auditing feature. It allows you to schedule and view compliance scans for any system.

SCAP content

SCAP content files defining the test rules can be created from scratch if you understand at least XCCDF or OVAL. XCCDF content is also frequently published online under open source licenses and this content can be customized to suit your needs.

The `openscap-content` package provides default content guidance for systems via a template.

 Note

SUSE supports the use of templates to evaluate your systems. However, you are creating custom content at your own risk.

SCAP was created to provide a standardized approach to maintaining system security, and the standards that are used will therefore continually change to meet the needs of the community and enterprise businesses. New specifications are governed by NIST's SCAP Release cycle in order to provide a consistent and repeatable revision work flow. For more information, see http://scap.nist.gov/timeline.html.

6.4.2 Prerequisites for Using OpenSCAP in SUSE Manager

The following sections describe the server and client prerequisites for using OpenSCAP.

Package Requirements

As Server: SUSE Manager 1.7 or later.

For the Client: `spacewalk-oscap` package (available from the SUSE Manager Tools Child Channel).

Entitlement Requirements

A Management entitlement is required for scheduling scans.

Other Requirements

Client: Distribution of the XCCDF content to all client machines.

You can distribute XCCDF content to client machines using any of the following methods:

- Traditional Methods (CD, USB, NFS, scp, ftp)

- SUSE Manager Scripts

- RPMs

Custom RPMs are the recommended way to distribute SCAP content to other machines. RPM packages can be signed and verified to ensure their integrity. Installation, removal, and verification of RPM packages can be managed from the user interface.

6.4.3 Performing Audit Scans

OpenSCAP integration in SUSE Manager provides the ability to perform audit scans on client systems. This section describes the available scanning methods.

PROCEDURE 6.1: SCANS VIA THE WEB INTERFACE

1. To perform a scan via the Web interface, log in to SUSE Manager.

2. Click on *Systems* and select the target system.

3. Click on *Audit ⟩ Schedule.*

4. Fill in the Schedule New XCCDF Scan form. See *Section 6.4.5.2.3, "Schedule Page"* for more information about the fields on this page.

 Warning

> The XCCDF content is validated before it is run on the remote system. Specifying invalid arguments can make spacewalk-oscap fail to validate or run. Due to security concerns the **oscap xccdf eval** command only accepts a limited set of parameters.

Run the **mgr_check** command to ensure the action is being picked up by the client system.

```
mgr_check -vv
```

 Note

> If the SUSE Manager daemon (**rhnsd**) or **osad** are running on the client system, the action will be picked up by these services. To check if they are running, use:
>
> ```
> service rhnsd start
> ```
>
> or
>
> ```
> service osad start
> ```

To view the results of the scan, refer to *Section 6.4.4, "Viewing SCAP Results".*

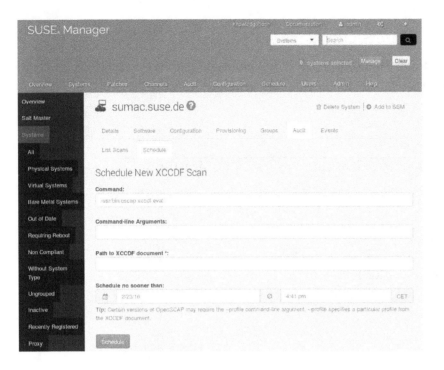

PROCEDURE 6.2: SCANS VIA API

1. To perform an audit scan via API, choose an existing script or create a script for scheduling a system scan through `system.scap.scheduleXccdfScan`, the front end API, for example:

```
#!/usr/bin/python
client = xmlrpclib.Server('https://spacewalk.example.com/rpc/api')
key = client.auth.login('username', 'password')
client.system.scap.scheduleXccdfScan(key, 1000010001,
    '/usr/local/share/scap/usgcb-sled11desktop-xccdf.xml',
    '--profile united_states_government_configuration_baseline')
```

Where:

- 1000010001 is the system ID (sid).

- /usr/local/share/scap/usgcb-sled11desktop-xccdf.xml is the path to the content location on the client system. In this case, it assumes USGCB content in the /usr/local/share/scap directory.

- --profile united_states_government_configuration_baseline is an additional argument for the **oscap** command. In this case, it is using the USGCB.

2. Run the script on the command-line interface of any system. The system needs the appropriate Python and XML-RPC libraries installed.

3. Run the **mgr_check** command to ensure that the action is being picked up by the client system.

```
mgr_check -vv
```

If the SUSE Manager daemon (**rhnsd**) or **osad** are running on the client system, the action will be picked up by these services. To check if they are running, use:

```
service rhnsd start
```

or

```
service osad start
```

 Note: Enabling Upload of Detailed SCAP Files

To make sure detailed information about the scan will be available, activate the upload of detailed SCAP files on the clients to be evaluated. On the *Admin* page, click on *Organization* and select one. Click on the *Configuration* tab and check *Enable Upload Of Detailed SCAP Files*. This feature generates an additional HTML version when you run a scan. The results will show an extra line like: Detailed Results: xccdf-report.html xccdf-results.xml scap-yast2sec-oval.xml.result.xml.

6.4.4 Viewing SCAP Results

There are three methods of viewing the results of finished scans:

- Via the Web interface. Once the scan has finished, the results should show up on the *Audit* tab of a specific system. This page is discussed in *Section 6.4.5, "OpenSCAP SUSE Manager Web Interface".*

- Via the API functions in handler `system.scap`.

- Via the **spacewalk-report** command as follows:

```
spacewalk-report system-history-scap
spacewalk-report scap-scan
spacewalk-report scap-scan-results
```

6.4.5 OpenSCAP SUSE Manager Web Interface

The following sections describe the tabs in the SUSE Manager Web interface that provide access to OpenSCAP and its features.

6.4.5.1 OpenSCAP Scans Page

Click the *Audit* tab on the top navigation bar, then OpenSCAP on the left. Here you can view, search for, and compare completed OpenSCAP scans.

6.4.5.1.1 *OpenSCAP > All Scans*

All Scans is the default page that appears on the *Audit › OpenSCAP* page. Here you see all the completed OpenSCAP scans you have permission to view. Permissions for scans are derived from system permissions.

For each scan, the following information is displayed:

System:
> the scanned system.

XCCDF Profile:
> the evaluated profile.

Completed:

> time of completion.

Satisfied:

> number of rules satisfied. A rule is considered to be satisfied if the result of the evaluation is either Pass or Fixed.

Dissatisfied:

> number of rules that were not satisfied. A rule is considered Dissatisfied if the result of the evaluation is a Fail.

Unknown:

> number of rules which failed to evaluate. A rule is considered to be Unknown if the result of the evaluation is an Error, Unknown or Not Checked.

The evaluation of XCCDF rules may also return status results like `Informational`, `Not Applicable`, or not `Selected`. In such cases, the given rule is not included in the statistics on this page. See *System Details > Audit* for information on these types of results.

6.4.5.1.2   OpenSCAP > XCCDF Diff

XCCDF Diff is an application that visualizes the comparison of two XCCDF scans. It shows metadata for two scans as well as the lists of results.

Click the appropriate icon on the Scans page to access the diff output of similar scans. Alternatively, specify the ID of scans you want to compare.

Items that show up in only one of the compared scans are considered to be "varying". Varying items are always highlighted in beige. There are three possible comparison modes:

Full Comparison

> all the scanned items.

Only Changed Items:

> items that have changed.

Only Invariant:

> unchanged or similar items.

6.4.5.1.3   *OpenSCAP > Advanced Search*

Use the Advanced Search page to search through your scans according to specified criteria including:

- rule results,

- targeted machine,

- time frame of the scan.

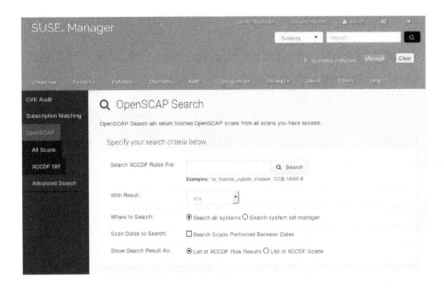

FIGURE 6.11: OPENSCAP ADVANCED SEARCH

The search either returns a list of results or a list of scans, which are included in the results.

6.4.5.2   Systems Audit Page

To display a system's audit page, click *Systems > system_name > Audit*. Use this page to schedule and view compliance scans for a particular system. Scans are performed by the OpenSCAP tool, which implements NIST's standard Security Content Automation Protocol (SCAP). Before you scan a system, make sure that the SCAP content is prepared and all prerequisites in *Section 6.4.2, "Prerequisites for Using OpenSCAP in SUSE Manager"* are met.

6.4.5.2.1 List Scans

This subtab lists a summary of all scans completed on the system. The following columns are displayed:

XCCDF Test Result

> The scan test result name, which provides a link to the detailed results of the scan.

Completed

> The exact time the scan finished.

Compliance

> The unweighted pass/fail ratio of compliance based on the Standard used.

P

> Number of checks that passed.

F

> Number of checks that failed.

E

> Number of errors that occurred during the scan.

U

> Unknown.

N

> Not applicable to the machine.

K

> Not checked.

S

> Not Selected.

I

> Informational.

X

> Fixed.

Total

> Total number of checks.

Each entry starts with an icon indicating the results of a comparison to a previous similar scan. The icons indicate the following:

- "RHN List Checked" Icon — no difference between the compared scans.

- "RHN List Alert" Icon — arbitrary differences between the compared scans.

- "RHN List Error" Icon — major differences between the compared scans. Either there are more failures than the previous scan or less passes

- "RHN List Check In" Icon — no comparable scan was found, therefore, no comparison was made.

To find out what has changed between two scans in more detail, select the ones you are interested in and click *Compare Selected Scans*. To delete scans that are no longer relevant, select those and click on *Remove Selected Scans*. Scan results can also be downloaded in CSV format.

6.4.5.2.2   Scan Details

The Scan Details page contains the results of a single scan. The page is divided into two sections:

Details of the XCCDF Scan

This section displays various details about the scan, including:

- File System Path: the path to the XCCDF file used for the scan.

- Command-line Arguments: any additional command-line arguments that were used.

- Profile Identifier: the profile identifier used for the scan.

- Profile Title: the title of the profile used for the scan.

- Scan's Error output: any errors encountered during the scan.

XCCDF Rule Results

The rule results provide the full list of XCCDF rule identifiers, identifying tags, and the result for each of these rule checks. This list can be filtered by a specific result.

6.4.5.2.3   Schedule Page

Use the Schedule New XCCDF Scan page to schedule new scans for specific machines. Scans occur at the system's next scheduled check-in that occurs after the date and time specified. The following fields can be configured:

Command-line Arguments:

Optional arguments to the `oscap` command, either:

- `--profile PROFILE`: Specifies a particular profile from the XCCDF document. Profiles are determined by the Profile tag in the XCCDF XML file. Use the `oscap` command to see a list of profiles within a given XCCDF file, for example:

```
# oscap info /usr/local/share/scap/dist_sles12_scap-sles12-oval.xml
Document type: XCCDF Checklist
Checklist version: 1.1
Status: draft
Generated: 2015-12-12
Imported: 2016-02-15T22:09:33
Resolved: false
Profiles: SLES12-Default
```

If not specified, the default profile is used. Some early versions of OpenSCAP in require that you use the `--profile` option or the scan will fail.

- `--skip-valid`: Do not validate input and output files. You can use this option to bypass the file validation process if you do not have well-formed XCCDF content.

Path to XCCDF Document:

This is a required field. The path parameter points to the XCCDF content location on the client system. For example: `/usr/local/scap/dist_rhel6_scap-rhel6-oval.xml`

 Warning

The XCCDF content is validated before it is run on the remote system. Specifying invalid arguments can cause **spacewalk-oscap** to fail to validate or run. Due to security concerns, the **oscap xccdf eval** command only accepts a limited set of parameters.

For information about how to schedule scans using the web interface, refer to *Procedure 6.1, "Scans via the Web Interface"*.

7 Configuration

Only Configuration Administrators or SUSE Manager Administrators see the *Configuration* tab.

In this configuration portal, manage your configuration channels and files centrally or limited to a single system. Centrally-managed files are available to multiple systems; changes to a single file affect all these systems.

7.1 Preparing Systems for Config Management

To manage a system's configuration with SUSE Manager, it must have the appropriate tools and the `config-enable` file installed. These tools should be available if you installed the system with the configuration management functionality using AutoYaST or Kickstart. If not, they can be found in the Tools child channel for your distribution. Download and install the latest `rhncfg*` packages:

- `rhncfg` — the base libraries and functions needed by all `rhncfg-*` packages,

- `rhncfg-actions` — the RPM package required to run configuration actions scheduled via SUSE Manager,

- `rhncfg-client` — the RPM package with a command line interface to the client features of the Configuration Management system,

- `rhncfg-management` — the RPM package with a command line interface used to manage SUSE Manager configuration.

First, enable your system to schedule configuration actions via Actions Control. Enter the **mgr-actions-control** command, provided by the `rhncfg-actions` RPM, on the client system to enable or disable specific actions.

7.2 Overview

The *Configuration Overview* shows all of the configuration files that are managed by your organization in SUSE Manager. This list includes files that are managed centrally in configuration channels and files that are managed locally via individual system profiles.

Configuration Summary

The panel provides quick information about your configuration files. Click on the blue text to the right to display relevant systems, channel details, or configuration files.

Configuration Actions

Configuration Actions offers direct access to the most common configuration management tasks. View or create files and channels or enable configuration management on your systems.

Recently Modified Configuration Files

The list shows which files have changed when and to which channel they belong. If no files have been changed, no list appears. Click on the name of a file to see its *Details* page. Click on the channel name to see its *Channel Details* page.

Recently Scheduled Configuration Deployments

Each scheduled action is listed along with the status of the action. Any scheduled configuration task, from enabling configuration management on a system to deploying a specific configuration file, is displayed. Here you can quickly assess if all tasks have been successfully carried out or fix any problems. Clicking on the blue text displays the *System Details > Schedule* page for the specified system.

7.3 Configuration Channels

As mentioned above, SUSE Manager manages both central and local configuration channels and files. Central configuration management allows you to deploy configuration files to multiple systems. Local configuration management allows you to specify overrides or configuration files that are not changed by subscribing the system to a central channel.

Central configuration channels must be created via the link on this page. Local configuration channels already exist for each system to which a Provisioning entitlement has been applied.

Click on the name of the configuration channel to see the details page for that channel. If you click on the number of files in the channel, you are taken to the *List/Remove Files* page of that channel. If you click on the number of systems subscribed to the configuration channel, you are taken to the *Systems > Subscribed Systems* page for that channel.

To create a new central configuration channel:

1. Click the *Create Config Channel* link in the upper right of this screen.

2. Enter a name for the channel.

3. Enter a label for the channel. This field must contain only alphanumeric characters, "-", "_", and ".".

4. Enter a mandatory description for the channel that allows you to distinguish it from other channels. No character restrictions apply.

5. Press the *Create Config Channel* button to create the new channel.

6. The following page is a subset of the *Channel Details* page and has three subtabs: *Overview*, *Add Files*, and *Systems*. The *Channel Details* page is discussed in *Section 7.3.1, "Configuration > Configuration Channels > Configuration Channel Details"*.

7.3.1   Configuration > Configuration Channels > Configuration Channel Details

Overview

This subtab is very similar to the *Configuration Overview* page. The *Channel Information* panel provides status information for the contents of the channel. The *Configuration Actions* panel provides access to the most common configuration tasks. The main difference is the *Channel Properties* panel. By clicking on the *Edit Properties* link, you can edit the name, label, and description of the channel.

List/Remove Files

This tab only appears if there are files in the configuration channel. You can remove files or copy the latest versions into a set of local overrides or into other central configuration channels. Check the box next to files you wish to manipulate and click the respective action button.

Add Files

The *Add Files* subtab has three subtabs of its own, which allow you to *Upload*, *Import*, or *Create* configuration files to be included in the channel.

Upload File

To upload a file into the configuration channel, browse for the file on your local system, populate all fields, and click the *Upload Configuration File* button. The *Filename/Path* field is the absolute path where the file will be deployed.

You can set the *Ownership* via the *user name* and *group name* as well as the *Permissions* of the file when it is deployed.

If the client has SELinux enabled, you can configure *SELinux contexts* to enable the required file attributes (such as user, role, and file type) that allow it to be used on the system.

If the configuration file includes a macro (a variable in a configuration file), enter the symbol that marks the beginning and end of the macro.

Import Files

To import files from other configuration channels, including any locally-managed channels, check the box to the left of any file you wish to import. Then press the *Import Configuration File(s)* button.

 Note

A sandbox icon indicates that the listed file is currently located in a local sandbox channel. Files in a system's sandbox channel are considered experimental and could be unstable. Use caution when selecting them for a central configuration channel.

Create File

Create a configuration file, directory, or symbolic link from scratch to be included in the configuration channel.

First, choose whether you want to create a text file, directory, or symbolic link (symlink) in the *File Type* section. In the `Filename/Path` text input field, set the absolute path to where the file should be deployed. If you are creating a symlink, indicate the target file and path in the *Symbolic Link Target Filename/Path* input field. Enter the *User name* and *Group name* for the file in the *Ownership* section, as well as the *File Permissions Mode*.

If the client has SELinux enabled, you can configure *SELinux contexts* to enable the required file attributes (such as user, role, and file type) that allow it to be used on the system.

If the configuration file includes a macro, enter the symbol that marks the beginning and end of the macro. Then enter the configuration file content in the *File Contents* field, using the script drop-down menu to choose the appropriate scripting language. Press the *Create Configuration File* button to create the new file.

Deploy Files

This subtab only appears when there are files in the channel and a system is subscribed to the channel. Deploy all files by clicking the *Deploy All Files* button or check selected files and click the *Deploy Selected Files* button. Select to which systems the file(s) should be applied. All systems subscribed to this channel are listed. If you wish to apply the file to a different system, subscribe it to the channel first. To deploy the files, press *Confirm & Deploy to Selected Systems*.

Systems

Manage systems subscribed to the configuration channel via two subtabs:

Subscribed Systems

All systems subscribed to the current channel are displayed. Click on the name of a system to see the *System Details* page.

Target Systems

This subtab displays a list of systems enabled for configuration management but not yet subscribed to the channel. To add a system to the configuration channel, check the box to the left of the system's name and press the *Subscribe System* button.

7.4 Configuration Files

This tab allows you to manage your configuration files independently. Both centrally-managed and locally-managed files can be reached from subtabs.

 Note

By default, the maximum file size for configuration files is 128KB (131072 bytes). If you need to change that value, check `web.maximum_config_file_size` in the `/usr/share/rhn/config-defaults/rhn_web.conf` file, and then set it in `/etc/rhn/rhn.conf` to the desired value. SUSE supports a configuration file size up to 1MB; larger values are not guaranteed to work.

You must also check `server.maximum_config_file_size` in the `/usr/share/rhn/config-defaults/rhn_server.conf` file and set it in `/etc/rhn/rhn.conf` to the same value as `web.maximum_config_file_size`.

Change the value of both the variables to the desired value in bytes in `/etc/rhn/rhn.conf`, e.g.:

```
server.maximum_config_file_size=262144
web.maximum_config_file_size=262144
```

7.4.1 Centrally-managed Files

Centrally-managed files are available to multiple systems. Changing a file within a centrally-managed channel may result in changes to several systems.

This page lists all files currently stored in your central configuration channel. Click on the *Path* of a file to see its *Configuration File Details* page. Click the name of the configuration channel to see its *Channel Details* page. Clicking on the number of systems shows you all systems currently subscribed to the channel containing that file. Click on the number of overriding systems to see all systems that have a local (or override) version of the configuration file. The centrally-managed file will not be deployed to those systems.

7.4.2 Locally-Managed Files

Locally-managed configuration files apply to only one system. They may be files in the system's sandbox or files that can be deployed to the system at any time. Local files have higher priority than centrally-managed files. If a system is subscribed to a configuration channel with a given file and also has a locally-managed version of that file, the locally-managed version will be deployed.

The list of all local (override) configuration files for your systems includes the local configuration channels and the sandbox channel for each Provisioning-entitled system.

Click the *Path* of the file to see its *Config File Details*. Click the name of the system to which it belongs to see its *System Details* > *Configuration* > *Overview* page.

7.4.3 Including Macros in your Configuration Files

Being able to store one file and share identical configurations is useful, but what if you have many variations of the same configuration file? What do you do if you have configuration files that differ only in system-specific details, such as host name and MAC address?

Traditional file management would require to upload and distribute each file separately, even if the distinction is nominal and the number of variations is in the hundreds or thousands. SUSE Manager addresses this by allowing the inclusion of macros, or variables, within the configuration files it manages. In addition to variables for custom system information, the following standard macros are supported:

- `rhn.system.sid`

- `rhn.system.profile_name`

- `rhn.system.description`

- `rhn.system.hostname`

- `rhn.system.ip_address`

- `rhn.system.custom_info(key_name)`

- `rhn.system.net_interface.ip_address(eth_device)`

- `rhn.system.net_interface.netmask(eth_device)`

- `rhn.system.net_interface.broadcast(eth_device)`

- `rhn.system.net_interface.hardware_address(eth_device)`

- `rhn.system.net_interface.driver_module(eth_device)`

To use this powerful feature, either upload or create a configuration file via the *Configuration Channel Details* page. Then open its *Configuration File Details* page and include the supported macros of your choice. Ensure that the delimiters used to offset your variables match those set in the *Macro Start Delimiter* and *Macro End Delimiter* fields and do not conflict with other characters in the file. We recommend that the delimiters be two characters in length and must not contain the percent (`%`) symbol.

For example, you may have a file applicable to all of your servers that differs only in IP address and host name. Rather than manage a separate configuration file for each server, you may create a single file, such as `server.conf`, with the IP address and host name macros included.

```
hostname={| rhn.system.hostname |}
ip_address={| rhn.system.net_interface.ip_address(eth0) |}
```

Upon delivery of the file to individual systems, whether through a scheduled action in the SUSE Manager Web interface or at the command line with the SUSE Manager Configuration Client (`mgrcfg-client`), the variables will be replaced with the host name and IP address of the system as recorded in SUSE Manager's system profile. In the above example configuration file the deployed version resembles the following:

```
hostname=test.example.domain.com
ip_address=177.18.54.7
```

To capture custom system information, insert the key label into the custom information macro (`rhn.system.custom_info`). For instance, if you developed a key labeled `"asset"` you can add it to the custom information macro in a configuration file to have the value substituted on any system containing it. The macro would look like this:

```
asset={@ rhn.system.custom_info(asset) @}
```

When the file is deployed to a system containing a value for that key, the macro gets translated, resulting in a string similar to the following:

```
asset=Example#456
```

To include a default value, for instance if one is required to prevent errors, you can append it to the custom information macro, like this:

```
asset={@ rhn.system.custom_info(asset) = 'Asset #' @}
```

This default is overridden by the value on any system containing it.

Using the SUSE Manager Configuration Manager (`mgrcfg-manager`) will not translate or alter files, as this tool is system agnostic. `mgrcfg-manager` does not depend on system settings. Binary files cannot be interpolated.

7.5 Systems

This page displays status information about your system in relation to configuration. There are two subtabs: *Managed Systems* and *Target Systems*.

7.5.1 Managed Systems

By default the *Configuration › Systems* page is displayed. The listed systems have been fully prepared for configuration file deployment. The number of local and centrally-managed files is displayed. Clicking the name of a system shows its *System Details › Configuration › Overview* page. Clicking on the number of local files takes you to the *System Details › Configuration › View/ Modify Files › Locally-Managed Files* page, where you manage which local (override) files apply to the system. Clicking on the number of centrally-managed files takes you to the *System Details › Configuration › Manage Configuration Channels › List/Unsubscribe from Channels* page. Here you unsubscribe from any channels you wish.

7.5.2 Target Systems

Here you see the systems either not prepared for configuration file deployment or not yet subscribed to a configuration channel. The table has three columns. The first identifies the system name, the second shows whether the system is prepared for configuration file deployment, and the third lists the steps necessary to prepare the system. To prepare a system, check the box to the left of the profile name then press the *Enable SUSE Manager Configuration Management* button. All of the preparatory steps that can be automatically performed are scheduled by SUSE Manager.

 Note

> You will have to perform some manual tasks to enable configuration file deployment. Follow the on-screen instructions provided to assist with each step.

8 Schedule

If you click the *Schedule* tab on the top navigation bar, the *Schedule* category and links appear. These pages enable you to track the actions carried out on your systems. An action is a scheduled task to be performed on one or more client systems. For example, an action can be scheduled to apply all patches to a system. Actions can also be grouped into action chains to schedule them at the same time in a particular order, for example to reboot a system after deploying patches.

SUSE Manager keeps track of the following action types:

1. package alteration (installation, upgrade, and removal),

2. rollback package actions,

3. system reboots,

4. patch application,

5. configuration file alteration (deploy, upload, and diff),

6. hardware profile updates,

7. package list profile updates,

8. automated installation initiation,

9. service pack migrations,

10. remote commands.

Each page in the *Schedule* category represents an action status.

8.1 Pending Actions

As shown in *Figure 8.1, "Schedule - Pending Actions"*, the **Pending Actions** page appears by default when clicking *Schedule* in the top navigation bar. It displays actions not yet started or still in progress.

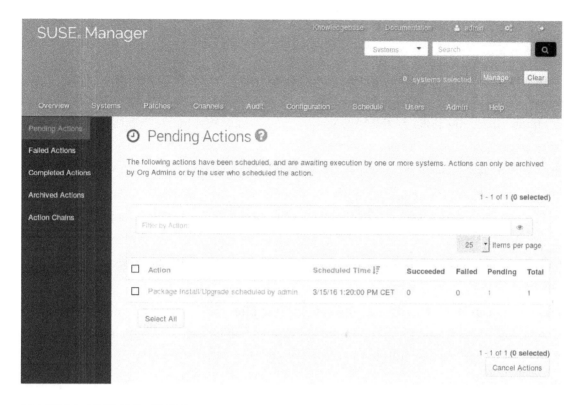

FIGURE 8.1: SCHEDULE - PENDING ACTIONS

8.2 Failed Actions

Sometimes actions cannot be completed. If the action returns an error, it is displayed here.

8.3 Completed Actions

List of actions successfully carried out.

8.4 Archived Actions

If you selected actions to store for review, they are displayed here and can be deleted.

8.5 Action Chains

All created action chains are displayed here and can be deleted or modified by clicking on the chain name. In the top right corner is the *delete action chain* link. To add actions to the selected chain, choose from the links at the top, leading to various "chainable" actions: *installing* or *upgrading* packages, running a *remote command* and *deploying a configuration file*. Additionally, packages can be removed or verified, patches applied and systems rebooted via action chains.

For all these operations, the action can either be scheduled for a certain date and time or added to an action chain. To create a new one, configure the first action (e.g. running a remote command), then select *Add to Action Chain* instead of *Schedule no sooner than:*. Click on the drop-down menu, enter a name, and click *Schedule* to save the chain. Then proceed to the next action and add it to the new chain.

An action chain can be executed on all the systems it applies to. If more than one action applies to the same system, corresponding supported operations will be executed sequentially in action chain order. If a supported operation fails on a system, no further supported operations will be executed on that system.

 Note

    SUSE Manager does not enforce ordering across different systems.

Action chains can be edited via the *Schedule › Action Chains* page. Click on a chain name to see the actions in the order they will be performed. The following tasks can be carried out here:

- Changing the order by dragging the respective action to the right position and dropping it.

- Deleting actions from the chain by clicking on the *delete action* link.

- Inspecting the list of systems on which an action is run by clicking on the + sign.

- Deleting a single system from an action by clicking on the *delete system* link.

- Deleting the complete chain with the *delete action chain* link in the top-left corner.

- Changing the action chain label by clicking on it.

- Scheduling the action chain for execution after a certain date by clicking on the *Save and Schedule* button.

Note

Note that if you leave the page without clicking on either *Save* or *Save and Schedule* all unsaved changes will be discarded. In this case, a confirmation dialog will pop up.

Currently you cannot add an action to an action chain from the *Edit* page. Once a Chain is scheduled, the actions it contains will be displayed under *Schedule* on the appropriate pages: *Pending Actions*, *Failed Actions* or *Completed Actions*, depending on the status. If one action fails on a system no other actions from the same chain will be executed on that systems. Due to technical limitations it is not possible to reuse Action Chains.

8.6   Actions List

On each action page, each row in the list represents a single scheduled event or action that might affect multiple systems and involve various packages. The list contains several columns of information:

- *Filter by Action* — Enter a term to filter the listed actions or use the check boxes in this column to select actions. Then either add them to your selection list or archive them by clicking *Archive Actions*. If you archive a pending action, it is not canceled, but the action item moves from the *Pending Actions* list to the *Archived Actions* list.

- *Action* — Type of action to perform such as Patches or Package Install. Clicking an action name shows its *Action Details* page. Refer to *Section 8.7, "Action Details"* for more information.

- *Scheduled Time* — The earliest day and time the action will be performed.

- *Succeeded* — Number of systems on which this action was successfully carried out.

- *Failed* — Number of systems on which this action has been tried and failed.

- *In Progress* — Number of systems on which this action is taking place.

- *Total* — Total number of systems on which this action has been scheduled.

8.7 Action Details

If you click on the name of an action, the *Action Details* page appears. This page is split into the following tabs:

8.7.1 Action Details > Details

General information about the action. This is the first tab you see when you click on an action. It displays the action type, scheduling administrator, earliest execution, and notes. Clicking the Patch Advisory takes you to the *Patch Details* page. The Patch Advisory appears only if the action is a patch. Refer to *Section 4.2.2, "Patch Details"* for more information.

8.7.2 Action Details > Completed Systems

List of systems on which the action has been successfully performed. Clicking a system name displays its *System Details* page. Refer to *Section 2.3, "System Details"* for more information.

8.7.3 Action Details > In Progress Systems

List of systems on which the action is now being carried out. To cancel an action, select the system by marking the appropriate check box and click the *Unschedule Action* button. Clicking a system name shows its *System Details* page. Refer to *Section 2.3, "System Details"* for more information.

8.7.4 Action Details > Failed Systems

List of systems on which the action has failed. It can be rescheduled here. Clicking a system name takes you to its *System Details* page. Refer to *Section 2.3, "System Details"* for more information.

8.7.5 Action Details > Package List

List of packages are associated with this action.

9 Users

Only SUSE Manager administrators can see the *Users* tab on the top navigation bar. If you click the tab, the *Users* category and links appear. Here you grant and edit permissions for those who administer your system groups. Click on a *Username* in the user list to modify the user.

To add new users to your organization, click the *Create User* link on the top right corner of the page. On the *Create User* page, fill in the required values for the new user.

Once all fields are completed, click the *Create Login* button. SUSE Manager now sends an email to the specified address and takes you back to the *Users › User List › Active* page. If you wish to set permissions and options for the new user, click on the name in the list. The *User Details* page for this user provides several subtabs of options. Refer to *Section 9.1.4, "User Details"* for detailed descriptions of each subtab.

9.1   User List

9.1.1   User List > Active

The user list shows all active users on your SUSE Manager and displays basic information about each user: username, real name, roles, and date of their last sign in.

As shown in *Figure 9.1, "User List"*, each row in the *User List* represents a user within your organization. There are four columns of information for each user:

- *Username* — The login name of the user. Clicking on a username, displays the *User Details* page for the user. Refer to *Section 9.1.4, "User Details"* for more information.

- *Real Name* — The full name of the user (last name first).

- *Roles* — List of the user's privileges, such as organization administrator, channel administrator and normal user. Users can have multiple roles.

- *Last Sign In* — Shows when the user last logged in to SUSE Manager.

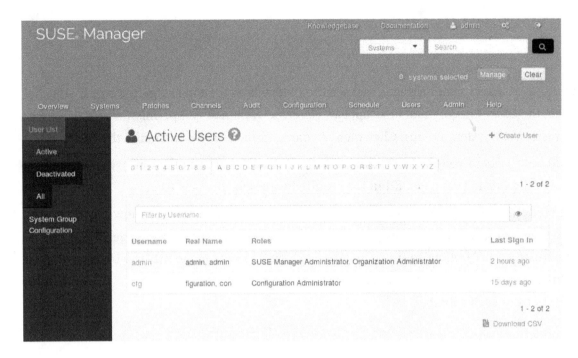

FIGURE 9.1: USER LIST

9.1.2   User List > Deactivated

The list of deactivated users also allows you to reactivate any of them. Click the check box to the left of their name and click the *Reactivate* button then the *Confirm* button. Reactivated users retain the permissions and system group associations they had when they were deactivated. Clicking a user name shows the *User Details* page.

9.1.3   User List > All

The *All* page lists all users that belong to your organization. In addition to the fields listed in the previous two screens, the table of users includes a *Status* field. This field indicates whether the user is *Active* or *Deactivated*. Deactivated users are also grayed out to indicate their status. Click on the user name to see the *User Details* page.

9.1.4   User Details

On the *User Details* page SUSE Manager, administrators manage the permissions and activity of all users. Here you can also delete or deactivate users.

Users can be deactivated directly in the SUSE Manager Web interface. SUSE Manager administrators can deactivate or delete users of their organization, but users can also deactivate their own accounts.

Deactivated users cannot log in to the SUSE Manager Web interface or schedule any actions. SUSE Manager administrators cannot be deactivated until that role is removed from their account. Actions scheduled by a user prior to their deactivation remain in the action queue. Deactivated users can be reactivated by SUSE Manager administrators.

 Warning: Irreversible Deletion

> User deletion is irreversible; exercise it with caution. Consider deactivating the user first in order to assess the effect deletion will have on your infrastructure.

To deactivate a user:

1. Click on a user name to navigate to the *User Details* tab.

2. Verify that the user is not a SUSE Manager administrator. If they are, uncheck the box to the left of that role and click the *Submit* button.

3. Click the *deactivate user* link in the upper right of the screen.

4. Click the *Deactivate User* button in the lower right to confirm.

To delete a user:

1. Click on a user name to navigate to the *User Details* tab.

2. Verify that the user is not a SUSE Manager administrator. Uncheck the box to remove the role if necessary.

3. Click the *Delete User* link in the upper right.

4. Click the *Delete User* button to permanently delete the user.

For instructions to deactivate your own account, refer to *Section 1.3.4, "Account Deactivation"*.

9.1.4.1 *User Details > Details*

This is the default *User Details* tab, which displays the username, first name, last name, email address, and roles of a user. Edit this information as needed and click *Update*. When changing a user's password, you will only see asterisks as you type.

To delegate responsibilities within your organization, SUSE Manager provides several roles with varying degrees of access. This list describes the permissions of each role and the differences between them:

- *User* (normal user) — Also known as a *System Group User*, this is the standard role associated with any newly created user. This person may be granted access to manage system groups and software channels, if the SUSE Manager administrator sets the roles accordingly. The systems must be in system groups for which the user has permissions to manage them. However, all globally subscribable channels may be used by anyone.

- *SUSE Manager Administrator* — This role allows a user to perform any function available in SUSE Manager. As the master account for your organization, the person holding this role can alter the privileges of all other accounts, as well as conduct any of the tasks available to the other roles. Like with other roles, multiple SUSE Manager administrators may exist. Go to *Admin › Users* and click the check box in the *SUSE Manager Admin?* row. *SUSE Manager Administrator* manages foreign organizations; for example, a *SUSE Manager Administrator* can only create users for an organization if he is entitled with organization administrator privileges for this organization.

- *Organization Administrator* — This role provides a user with all the permissions other administrators have, namely the activation key, configuration, channel, and system group administrator.

- *Activation Key Administrator* — This role is designed to manage your collection of activation keys. A user assigned to this role can modify and delete any key within your organization.

- *Configuration Administrator* — This role enables a user to manage the configuration of systems within the organization, using either the SUSE Manager Web interface or the `rhncfg-management`.

- *Channel Administrator* — This role provides a user with full access to all software channels within your organization. This requires the SUSE Manager synchronization tool (`mgr-sync`). The channel administrator may change the base channels of systems, make channels globally subscribable, and create entirely new channels.

- *System Group Administrator* — This role is one step below SUSE Manager administrator: full authority is limited to systems or system groups to which access is granted. The System Group Administrator can create new system groups, delete any assigned systems from groups, add systems to groups, and manage user access to groups.

Being a SUSE Manager administrator enables you to remove administrator rights from other users. It is possible to remove your own privileges as long as you are not the only SUSE Manager administrator.

To assign a new role to a user, check the respective box. SUSE Manager administrators are automatically granted administration access to all other roles, signified by grayed-out check boxes. Click *Update* to submit your changes.

9.1.4.2 *User Details > System Groups*

This tab displays a list of system groups the user may administer; for more information about system groups, see *Section 2.4, "System Groups"*. SUSE Manager administrators can set this user's access permissions to each system group. Check or uncheck the box to the left of the system group and click the *Update Permissions* button to save the changes.

SUSE Manager administrators may select one or more default system groups for a user. When the user registers a system, it gets assigned to the selected group or groups. This allows the user to access the newly-registered system immediately. System groups to which this user has access are preceded by an (*).

9.1.4.3 *User Details > Systems*

This tab lists all systems a user can access according to the system groups assigned to the user. To carry out tasks on some of these systems, select the set of systems by checking the boxes to the left and click the *Update List* button. Use the System Set Manager page to execute actions on those systems. Clicking the name of a system takes you to its *System Details* page. Refer to *Section 2.3, "System Details"* for more information.

9.1.4.4 *User Details > Channel Permissions*

This tab lists all channels available to your organization. Grant explicit channel subscription permission to a user for each of the channels listed by checking the box to the left of the channel, then click the *Update Permissions* button. Permissions granted by a SUSE Manager administrator or channel administrator have no check box but a check icon just like globally subscribable channels.

9.1.4.4.1 *User Details > Channel Permissions > Subscription*

Identifies channels to which the user may subscribe systems. To change these, select or deselect the appropriate check boxes and click the *Update Permissions* button. Note that channels subscribable due to the user's administrator status or the channel's global settings cannot be altered. They are identified with a check icon.

9.1.4.4.2 *User Details > Channel Permissions > Management*

Identifies channels the user may manage. To change these, select or deselect the appropriate check boxes and click the *Update Permissions* button. The permission to manage channels does not enable the user to create new channels. Note that channels automatically manageable through the user's admin status cannot be altered. These channels are identified with a check icon. Remember, SUSE Manager administrators and channel administrators can subscribe to or manage any channel.

9.1.4.5 *User Details > Preferences*

Configure the following settings for the user:

- *Email Notifications*: Determine whether this user should receive email every time a patch alert is applicable to one or more systems in his or her SUSE Manager account, as well as daily summaries of system events.

- *SUSE Manager List Page Size*: Maximum number of items that appear in a list on a single page. If the list contains more items than can be displayed on one page, click the *Next* button to see the next page. This preference applies to the user's view of system lists, patch lists, package lists, and so on.

- *Overview Start Page*: Configure which information to be displayed on the "Overview" page at login.

- *CSV Files*: Select whether to use the default comma or a semicolon as separator in downloadable CSV files.

Change these options to fit your needs, then click the *Save Preferences* button. To change the time zone for this user, click on the *Locale* subtab and select from the drop-down menu. Dates and times, like system check-in times, will be displayed according to the selected time zone. Click *Save Preferences* for changes to take effect.

9.1.4.6 User Details > Addresses

This tab lists mailing addresses associated with the user's account. If there is no address specified yet, click *Fill in this address* and fill out the form. When finished, click *Update*. To modify this information, click the *Edit this address* link, change the relevant information, and click the *Update* button.

9.2 System Group Configuration

10 Admin

The *Admin* page allows SUSE Manager customers to manage the basic configuration, including creating and managing multiple organizations. Only the SUSE Manager administrator can access the *Admin* page.

10.1 *Admin > Setup Wizard*

Setting up SUSE Manager typically requires some extra steps after installation for common configuration tasks.

The *Setup Wizard* link is displayed when the SUSE Manager Web interface is used for the fist time and can be accessed later at any time by clicking on *Admin › Setup Wizard*. On the three tabs configure the HTTP proxy server, organization credentials, and SUSE products.

HTTP Proxy:

Configure a proxy server that SUSE Manager will use to access SCC (SUSE Customer Center) and other remote servers here. Use `hostname:port` syntax in the *Hostname* field if the proxy port is not 80. Clearing the fields disables proxy.

Organization Credentials:

Click *Add a new credential* and enter username and password to allow a user to access SCC. After saving, a new credential card will be displayed. Buttons below the credential card allow you to:

- see the credential validation status (green tick or red cross icon). To re-check the credential with SCC, click on the icon;

- set the primary credentials for inter-server synchronization (yellow star icon);

- list the subscriptions related to a certain credential (list icon);

- edit the credential (pencil icon);

- delete the credential (trash can icon).

SUSE Products:

On the *SUSE Products* page, select product-specific channels you are entitled to. The products displayed are directly linked to your organization credentials as well as your SUSE subscriptions. Product extentions and modules are shown when you select the corresponding base product or click the plus sign to its left. After you have made your selection, click *Add products*. This equals running the `mgr-sync add products` command.

 Note

> Channel synchronization will take place and might take several hours. Afterward the corresponding channels can be used in SUSE Manager.

Alternatively, you can add listed channels right away by clicking the *Add this product* button in the status column. A progress bar will be displayed. Now you can select add-on products requiring the product that is currently added. To check for required products, click on the list icon in the *Channels* column. Once a product is downloaded and ready to use, the state will change to *Finished*.

10.2   Admin > Organizations

The multiple organizations feature allows administrators to create and manage multiple organizations across SUSE Manager. Administrators can allocate software and system entitlements across various organizations, as well as control an organization's access to system management tasks.

If you click on the name of an organization, the Organization Details page appears.

10.2.1   Organization Details > Details

This screen lists the details of an organization.

10.2.2   Organization Details > Users

List of all the users of an organization. You can can modify the user details if you are logged into that organization and have organization administrator privileges.

10.2.3 Organization Details > Trust

10.2.4 Organization Details > Configuration

Here you configure the organization to use staging contents, set up software crash reporting, and upload of SCAP files. Crash file and SCAP file upload limit is a non negative number, zero means no limit.

Staging means that clients will download packages in advance. Then the package installation action will take place immediately, when the schedule is actually executed. This "pre-fetching" saves maintenance window time, which is good for service uptime.

For staging contents, edit on the client `/etc/sysconfig/rhn/up2date`:

```
stagingContent=1
stagingContentWindow=24
```

`stagingContentWindow` is a time value expressed in hours that determines when the downloading should start. More exactly it is the number of hours before the scheduled installation or update time. In this case, 24 hours before the installation time. The exact download start time depends on the contact method—basically at the next **rhn_check**.

Next time a package installation, update, or patch application action is scheduled, packages will be automatically downloaded but not installed yet. When the scheduled time comes, the action will attempt to use the staged version.

10.3 Admin > Users

To view and manage all users of the organization you are currently logged in to, click *Users* in the left navigation bar. The table lists username, real name, organization and whether the user is organization or SUSE Manager administrator. To modify administrator privileges, click on the username to get to the user's *Details* page.

10.4 Admin > SUSE Manager Configuration

This tab is split into subtabs that allow you to configure most aspects of SUSE Manager. If you change the configuration, restart SUSE Manager on the final tab for the changes to take effect.

10.4.1 Admin > SUSE Manager Configuration > General

This page allows you to alter the most basic settings, such as the admin email address or a proxy configuration.

10.4.2 Admin > SUSE Manager Configuration > Bootstrap Script

The *SUSE Manager Configuration › Bootstrap Script* page allows you to generate a bootstrap script for redirecting client systems from the central SUSE Customer Center to SUSE Manager. This script, to be placed in the `/srv/www/htdocs/pub/bootstrap/` directory of SUSE Manager, significantly reduces the effort involved in reconfiguring all systems, which by default obtain packages from the central SUSE Customer Center. The required fields are pre-populated with values derived from previous installation steps. Ensure this information is accurate.

Check boxes offer options for including built-in security SSL and GNU Privacy Guard (GPG) features, both of which are advised. In addition, you may enable remote command acceptance and remote configuration management of the systems to be bootstrapped here. Both features are useful for completing client configuration. Finally, if you are using an HTTP proxy server, fill in the related fields. When finished, click *Update*.

10.4.3 Admin > SUSE Manager Configuration > Organizations

The *SUSE Manager Configuration › Organizations* page contains details about the organizations feature of SUSE Manager, as well as links to quickly get started creating and configuring organizations.

10.4.4 Admin > SUSE Manager Configuration > Restart

The *SUSE Manager Configuration › Restart* page comprises the final step in configuring SUSE Manager. Click the *Restart* button to restart SUSE Manager and incorporate all of the configuration options added on the previous screens. It will take between four and five minutes for the restart to finish.

10.4.5 Admin > SUSE Manager Configuration > Cobbler

On the *SUSE Manager Configuration › Cobbler* page you can run the Cobbler Sync by clicking *Update*. Cobbler Sync is used to repair or rebuild the contents of `/srv/tftpboot` or `/srv/www/cobbler` when a manual modification of the cobbler setup has occurred.

10.4.6 Admin > SUSE Manager Configuration > Bare-metal systems

Here you can add unprovisioned ("bare-metal") systems capable of PXE booting to an organization. After that happens, those systems will appear in the *Systems* list, where regular provisioning via autoinstallation is possible in a completely unattended fashion. Only x86_64 systems with at least 1 GB of RAM are supported. SUSE Manager server will use its integrated Cobbler instance and will act as TFTP server for this feature to work, so the network segment that connects it to target systems must be properly configured. In particular, a DHCP server must exist and have a next-server configuration parameter set to the SUSE Manager server IP address or hostname.

Once enabled, any bare-metal system connected to the SUSE Manager server network will be automatically added to the organization when it powers on. The process typically takes a few minutes; when it finishes, the system will automatically shut down and then appear in the *Systems* list.

 Note

Note that new systems will be added to the organization of the administrator who enabled this feature. To change the organization, disable the feature, log in as an administrator of a different organization and enable it again.

Provisioning can be initiated by clicking on the Provisioning tab. In case of bare-metal systems, though, provisioning cannot be scheduled, it will happen automatically as soon as it is completely configured and the system is powered on.

It is possible to use *System Set Manager* with bare-metal systems, although in that case some features will not be available as those systems do not have an operating system installed. This limitation also applies to mixed sets with regular and bare-metal systems: full features will be enabled again once all bare-metal systems are removed from the set.

10.5 Admin > ISS Configuration

Inter-Server Synchronization (ISS) allows a SUSE Manager to synchronize content and permissions from another SUSE Manager instance in a peer-to-peer relationship.

10.5.1 Configuring the Master SUSE Manager Server

Click *Admin ›* > *ISS Configuration* › *Master Setup*. In the top right-hand corner of this page, click *Add New Slave* and fill in the following information:

- Slave Fully Qualified Domain Name (FQDN)

- Allow Slave to Sync? — Choosing this field will allow the slave SUSE Manager to access this master SUSE Manager. Otherwise, contact with this slave will be denied.

- Sync All Orgs to Slave? — Checking this field will synchronize all organizations to the slave SUSE Manager.

 Note

Choosing the *Sync All Orgs to Slave?* option on the *Master Setup* page will override any specifically selected organizations in the local organization table.

Click Create. Optionally, click on any local organization to be exported to the slave SUSE Manager then click *Allow Orgs*.

To enable the inter-server synchronization (ISS) feature, edit the `/etc/rhn/rhn.conf` file and set: `disable_iss=0`. Save the file and restart the httpd service with `service httpd restart`.

10.5.2 Configuring Slave Servers

Slave servers receive content synchronized from the master server. To securely transfer content to the slave servers, the ORG-SSL certificate from the master server is needed. Click on *Admin > ISS Configuration > Slave Setup*. In the top right-hand corner, click *Add New Master* and fill in the following information:

- Master Fully Qualified Domain Name (FQDN)

- Default Master?

- Filename of this Master's CA Certificate: use the full path to the CA Certificate.

Click Add New Master.

Once the master and slave servers are configured, a synchronization can be performed by running the **mgr-inter-sync** command:

```
mgr-inter-sync -c YOUR-CHANNEL
```

10.5.3 Mapping SUSE Manager Master Server Organizations to Slave Organizations

A mapping between organizational names on the master SUSE Manager allows for channel access permissions to be set on the master server and propagated when content is synced to a slave SUSE Manager. Not all organization and channel details need to be mapped for all slaves. SUSE Manager administrators can select which permissions and organizations can be synchronized by allowing or omitting mappings.

To complete the mapping, log in to the Slave SUSE Manager as administrator. Click on *Admin > ISS Configuration > Slave Setup* and select a master SUSE Manager by clicking on its name. Use the drop-down box to map the exported master organization name to a matching local organization in the slave SUSE Manager, then click *Update Mapping*.

On the command line, issue the synchronization command on each of the custom channels to obtain the correct trust structure and channel permissions:

```
mgr-inter-sync -c YOUR-CHANNEL
```

10.6 Admin > Task Schedules

Under *Task Schedules* all predefined task bunches are listed. Click on a schedule name to disable it or change the frequency. Click on *Edit Schedule* to update the schedule with your settings. To delete a schedule, click on *delete schedule* in the upper right-hand corner.

 Warning

> Only disable or delete a schedule if you are absolutely certain this is necessary as they are essential for SUSE Manager to work properly.

If you click on a bunch name, a list of runs of that bunch type and their status will be displayed. Clicking on the start time links takes you back to the *Basic Schedule Details*.

The following predefined task bunches are scheduled by default and can be configured:

channel-repodata-default:

> (re)generates repository metadata files.

cleanup-data-default:

> cleans up stale package change log and monitoring time series data from the database.

clear-taskologs-default:

> clears task engine (taskomatic) history data older than a specified number of days, depending on the job type, from the database.

cobbler-sync-default:

> syncs distribution and profile data from SUSE Manager to Cobbler.

compare-configs-default:

> compares configuration files as stored in configuration channels with the files stored on all configuration-enabled servers. To review comparisons, click on the *Systems* tab and click on the system of interest. Go to *Configuration › Compare Files*. For more information, refer to *Section 2.3.3.5, " System Details > Configuration > Compare Files ".*

cve-server-channels-default:

> updates internal pre-computed CVE data that is used to display results on the *CVE Audit* page. Search results in the *CVE Audit* page are updated to the last run of this schedule). For more information, see *Section 6.1, "CVE Audit".*

daily-status-default:

> sends daily report emails to relevant addresses. See *Section 9.1.4.5, "User Details > Preferences"* to learn more about how to configure notifications for specific users.

errata-cache-default:

> updates internal patch cache database tables, which are used to look up packages that need updates for each server. Also, this sends notification emails to users that might be interested in certain patches. For more information on patches, see *Chapter 4, Patches*.

errata-queue-default:

> queues automatic updates (patches) for servers that are configured to receive them.

kickstart-cleanup-default:

> cleans up stale kickstart session data.

kickstartfile-sync-default:

> generates Cobbler files corresponding to Kickstart profiles created by the configuration wizard.

mgr-register-default:

> calls the `mgr-register` command, which synchronizes client registration data with NCC (new, changed or deleted clients' data are forwarded).

package-cleanup-default:

> deletes stale package files from the file system.

reboot-action-cleanup-default:

> any reboot actions pending for more than six hours are marked as failed and associated data is cleaned up in the database. For more information on scheduling reboot actions, see *Section 2.3.4.2, " System Details > Provisioning > Power Management "*.

sandbox-cleanup-default:

> cleans up *sandbox* configuration files and channels that are older than the *sandbox_lifetime* configuration parameter (3 days by default). Sandbox files are those imported from systems or files under development. For more information, see *Section 2.3.3.3, " System Details > Configuration > Add Files "*

session-cleanup-default:

> cleans up stale Web interface sessions, typically data that is temporarily stored when a user logs in and then closes the browser before logging out.

ssh-push-default:

prompts clients to check in with SUSE Manager via SSH if they are configured with a *SSH Push* contact method.

10.7 Admin > Task Engine Status

Here you can keep track of all scheduled tasks run by the SUSE Manager task engine. Next to the task name you find the date and time of the last execution and the status.

10.8 Admin > Show Tomcat Logs

You can access Tomcat logs by clicking on the *Show Tomcat Logs* link.

11 Help

The *Help* pages provide access to the full suite of documentation and support available to SUSE Manager users. Click *Help* in the *Overview* category to see a list of options available to you.

11.1 SUSE Manager Getting Started Guide

The SUSE Manager Getting Started Guide provides information regarding SUSE Manager server and its installation and initial configuration. Implementing a fully functional SUSE Manager requires more than installing software and a database. Client systems must be configured to use SUSE Manager. Custom packages and channels should be created for optimal use. Since these tasks extend beyond the basic installation, they are covered in detail in the other guides.

11.2 SUSE Manager Reference Guide

The *SUSE Manager Reference Guide* explains the Web interface and its features in detail.

11.3 SUSE Manager Best Practices Guide

The *SUSE Manager Best Practices Guide* describes SUSE recommended best practices for SUSE Manager. This information has been collected from a large number of successful SUSE Manager real world implementations and includes feedback provided by product management, sales, and engineering.

11.4 SUSE Manager Advanced Topics Guide

The *SUSE Manager Advanced Topics Guide* contains a collection of advanced topics not covered under the best practices guide. For example, *Book "Advanced Topics", Chapter 1 "SUSE Manager on IBM z Systems "*.

11.5   Release Notes

The *Release Notes* page lists the notes accompanying every recent release of SUSE Manager. All significant changes occurring in a given release cycle, from major enhancements to the user interface to changes in the related documentation are documented here.

11.6   Search

The *Documentation Search* page features a robust search engine that indexes and searches SUSE Manager documentation.

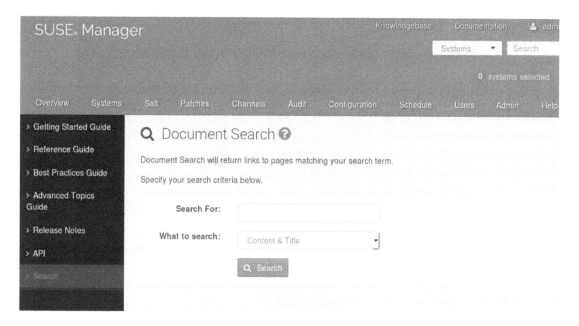

FIGURE 11.1: DOCUMENTATION SEARCH

Users can search the available online documentation and filter them according to the following choices in the *What to Search* drop-down menu:

- *Content & Title* — Search both the title heading or body content of all available documents.

- *Free Form* — Search documents and indices for any keyword matches, which broadens search results.

- *Content* — Search only the body content of documentation for more specific matches.

- *Title* — Search only the title headings of the documentation for targeted, specific search results.

The *Free Form* field additionally allows you to search using field names that you prepend to search queries and filter results in that field.

For example, if you wanted to search all of the SUSE Manager manuals for the word `Virtualization` in the title and `install` in the content, type the following in the *Free Form* field:

```
title:Virtualization and content:install
```

Other supported field names for documentation search include:

- `url` — Search the URL for a particular keyword.

- `title` — Search titles for a particular keyword.

- `content` — Search the body of the documentation for a particular keyword.

If there are several pages of search results, you can limit the amount of visible results shown on one page by clicking the *Display quantity items per page* drop-down menu, which offers between 10 and 500 results per page.

To move between pages, click the right or left angle brackets (> to go forward or < to go backward).

II Command Line Interface

12 Command Line Administration

III Glossary

Glossary Database

This is not a real glossary, it's just an example.

Extensible Markup Language
> The definition of the XML language goes here.